For those seeking to participate in God's mi
opment, this instructive book is gold! Tim M
an invaluable resource packed with wisdom
missionary work in Eastern Africa. The boc
challenges that face the church and African communities today. Grounding
his missional approach in biblical exposition, Tim highlights opportunities
and effective ideas for the church to be involved in community development,
and in so doing equips pastors and lay Christians for integral mission in their
communities.

Robert Falconer, PhD
Coordinator of Student Research,
South African Theological Seminary, Johannesburg

Tim Monger has gifted us with a powerful, inspiring book about the distinc-
tive role of community transformation within the holistic mission of God
and thus within the church's holistic, integrated mission. Writing from years
of experience, he offers a robustly biblical and highly practical perspective
that speaks from and to the African context – and beyond. (The treatment of
Genesis and community development, for instance, is brilliant.) As he emphasizes, the transforming church will itself be the church transformed. Highly
recommended!

Michael J. Gorman, PhD
Raymond E. Brown Professor of Biblical Studies and Theology,
St. Mary's Seminary & University, Maryland, USA

It is relatively easy to make the case that local churches are called to participate
in the upliftment of their communities as an expression of their participation
in God's mission. How this might happen is the more difficult question. Tim
Monger helps us here. He has written a book that brings together his experience, study and thoughtful reflection on this question. It will be a great aid to
students, church leaders and development practitioners of church-facilitated
community development.

Deborah Hancox, PhD
International Coordinator,
Micah Global, South Africa

As one born and mostly raised in Africa, and deeply passionate for its church and its peoples, reading about the ministry in this book brought joy and hope. Its praxis fleshes out the very essence of mission as participation in the mission of the triune God – mission both deep and wide, and mission that includes evangelism, justice and human flourishing. Its culturally sensitive, communal, holistic, incarnational and pneumatic approach is a corrective for all dualistic, imperialist and unsustainable approaches to mission. I highly recommend it!

Ross Hastings, PhD
Sangwoo Youtong Chee Professor of Theology,
Regent College, Canada

Despite the many challenges facing her, the church in Africa has been growing in numbers at a tremendous pace and for this we must give all the glory to the head of the church, Jesus Christ, who alone gives the increase. Evangelism and church planting have been the top two items on the agenda of the church in Africa. Much of the training that takes place in the various Bible schools and seminaries is designed to produce church ministers who shall do evangelism and church planting on the continent.

But God has a larger purpose and a wider mission than that – to transform holistically the society in which the church is planted. So will the church in Africa take up this mantle? That is the most important question posed in this book.

We must reset how we do church. We must rethink our current programmes so as to embrace God's larger purpose and wider mission. Then we will plant community transforming churches that are salt and light in the community.

In this book, *Transforming Church*, borne out of real life experiences on the mission field in the twenty-first century and lots of research, Tim Monger has presented a great starting point for purposeful discussion for church leaders all over Africa with a view of changing the way we have done church and missions to date.

Africa, let us "take up the mantle" and "go for God's larger purpose and wider mission" lest we become salt that has lost its saltiness.

Bishop John B. Masinde
Senior Pastor, Deliverance Church International, Umoja
General Secretary, Deliverance Church, Kenya

Africa's time for playing a leading role in Christianity has come. Millions are coming to Christ and the centre of Christianity is shifting towards Africa. It is vital therefore that the church in Africa takes the good news of Jesus Christ into every sphere to bring about a thorough transformation of society. I commend *Transforming Church* as a book to help the church to fulfil this vision through its life, words and action, and be used by God to bring life in all its fullness to our communities. As the church in Africa lives out this vision, it will bring immense blessing to Africa and be a provocative example to the church in the rest of the world.

Barnabas Mtokambali, DMin
Archbishop of Tanzania Assemblies of God

Tim Monger has written an excellent book, that should be on every pastor, theologian, community development specialist and ordinary Christian's bookshelf. It addresses the concept of integral mission in a very accessible yet well researched way. Integral mission in Monger's understanding is the backbone for community development. The reality of poverty requires the church to develop the community. Monger understands the reason for poverty. He is aware of the complex issues behind why people are poor and it is with this background that he suggests how the church can carry out integral mission. The book strikes a balance that is both academic and practical, something that scholars rarely manage to do. Monger has learnt how to engage in integral mission in Tanzania where he has worked with the church to carry out some of the projects he offers as examples in this book. The ideas in this book are not ivory tower ideas; they come from a theologian with a heart for the community. Monger desires to see our theology lived out in the life of the church. It is from that perspective that he presents the practical guidelines on how to design a project and execute it, while at the same time partnering with God. There is much in this book that can help the church in Africa to fulfil God's mission. I highly recommend this book and I hope it will be used by the African church in its quest to fulfil God's mission on the continent.

Gift Mtukwa, PhD
Chair of Department of School of Religion and Christian Ministry,
Africa Nazarene University, Kenya

This challenging and informative book is deeply rooted in the biblical narratives reflecting God's redemptive, healing and renewing passion for the world. It embodies the experience of the African church in being a sign and servant of God's purposes, including in the restorative work of church-based community development. This book can serve as a profound resource as the church seeks to be God's renewing good news in the world, bringing healing, justice, "bread" on the table, and peace in the community.

Charles Ringma, PhD
Emeritus Professor of Missions and Evangelism,
Regent College, Canada

Birthed in costly mission, and combining Scripture, Spirit and experience, this informed, accessible, practical and above all deeply pastoral book has something for all churches everywhere who are seeking to transform their communities with the life of God.

Rikk Watts, PhD
Research Professor of New Testament,
Regent College, Canada

Transforming Church

Langham
GLOBAL LIBRARY

Transforming Church

Participating in God's Mission through
Community Development

Tim Monger

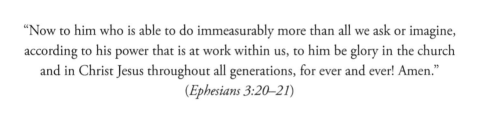

"Now to him who is able to do immeasurably more than all we ask or imagine, according to his power that is at work within us, to him be glory in the church and in Christ Jesus throughout all generations, for ever and ever! Amen."
(*Ephesians 3:20–21*)

Contents

Foreword

We Africans and African Christian leaders know all too well the challenges and struggles of Africa today. We see them every day. And we also know the immense calling God has for his church to proclaim the good news of Jesus and see his kingdom and wisdom come in every place in society. But how can the African church be effective in this task and offer real hope among the day-to-day challenges and struggles of its communities?

The church must be transformed from the inside out in order to be transforming. We must see that the life of the church in all its aspects is missional and that God calls us to embrace his holistic mission as he is concerned with the whole person, the whole community: body, mind and spirit. This means that to be true to the Bible, to follow the example of Jesus, the church must address the whole person and whole community in all their needs. This has implications for the individual Christian, for the local church, for denominations and church groups, for missionary societies, for Christian NGOs and for theological training institutions.

Tim Monger partnered with our family of churches in the Mwanza region of Tanzania as we began this journey of growing into holistic or integral mission. He, his wife Rachel and their daughters Amisadai and Louisa lived and worked with us. As a family, they lived an ordinary life, adapted to the Tanzanian environment and served together, making many sacrifices to make sure that less-privileged people and families including children with albinism were reached.

Tim is known to be a leader full of God's grace and wisdom. He is a preacher of the gospel of Jesus reaching many people with the word of God and showing how it connects with daily life. But he is also a practical trainer as he teaches what he lives, adjusting quickly to Tanzanian culture and learning our language. He helped us introduce sustainable agricultural skills to our student pastors in church-planting schools which has led them into a more effective ministry. But he and his team also helped us begin beekeeping, girls' menstrual health, community health education and entrepreneurship projects, sometimes in the farthest places. All these enabled the church to bring to many communities spiritual, physical, psychological and even economic benefits.

Tim has enabled Emmanuel International to be recognized as the co-worker with Tanzania Assemblies of God (TAG) in integral mission. Emmanuel

International is recognized by TAG national office and is now helping TAG in another region with particular challenges to reach the predominantly Muslim population through integral mission and practical projects.

As Christianity in Africa comes of age, may the church be enabled to bring about a lasting and wide gospel transformation so Africa can enjoy living under the reign of God. And so I heartily recommend this book, *Transforming Church: Participating in God's Mission Through Community Development.*

Valentine Mbuke
Assistant Bishop of South Mwanza District,
National Leader of Teen Challenge, Tanzania
September 2021

Preface

This book comes out of many years of living in Tanzania and serving with churches to assist them to be equipped for integral mission in their communities. My work with the churches consisted of biblical training in mission, practical training in community development projects and seeking to put these two together into a unified whole. My time in Tanzania was a journey of discovery, attempting, making mistakes, listening and learning. The church's workers and I found no well-worn paths or methods for doing this work, but discovered that, though there are many pitfalls, if we are faithful, wise and willing to learn, God can lead us to work effectively with the African church so that it is shaped to participate in a mission of community transformation.

I have written this work to pass on what I have learned in seeking to implement practically a theological vision of church-based mission, rooted in the biblical story and relevant for today. Theology and practice must go hand in hand. God's mission is always profound and deep and at the same time always relevant and practical. Community development among poor communities is a vital outworking of the gospel, concretely revealing the wisdom, power and love of God.

This is a book for students, pastors and Christian development workers (local or expatriate), involved, or seeking to be involved, in rural or urban community development in Africa, to help them think theologically and culturally about their work. It is heartening to see a shift taking place in community development in Africa, where African churches themselves are increasingly taking up the mantle to undertake this vital work. The church is after all the people charged by God to partner with him in bringing his kingdom into every sphere of life, with Jesus enthroned as Lord over all. But often we can be unreflective about this work, doing what comes naturally, following "accepted" development theories, being at the mercy of donors and their agendas, or not sure how community development quite fits into the overall mission of the church. No wonder there is often a lack of whole-life transformation, empowerment and sustainability of the work! But this need not be the case.

This book then is an attempt to show the reader how community development can be conducted within the overall mission of the church and explicitly connected to this mission. In this way community development and mission are mutually enhancing, and the church is empowered to participate more fully in God's mission to renew and transform all creation. We consider vital components to community development that must be reflected upon theologically and culturally to ensure we are living and working within a proper missional framework. The aim is not to prescribe a method to follow but to give Christian workers the vital tools to be able to think biblically, culturally and relevantly so as to design and conduct a contextualized transformative approach to community development for the churches in their localities. Then, even if a church involves other actors in supporting this work, the church itself through the power of the Holy Spirit will be the driver of change.

It may help if I provide some background to me and my work in Africa, since I refer to it throughout, sometimes positively and sometimes less so, as a means of grounding the discussion or offering examples to reflect upon. My family and I served with Emmanuel International, a Christian organization which partners with churches to serve the poor in holistic mission. We began in Iringa, Tanzania, partnering with the Anglican Diocese of Ruaha, assisting them to set up a fuel-efficient stoves project in the villages of Magozi and Kimande. During this time, we also partnered with the Pentecostal Holiness Mission, Iringa District, for which I taught missiology courses in their Bible college.

After this, at the request of the Tanzania Assemblies of God bishop of Mwanza, we moved to Mwanza to help them develop a holistic approach to mission across the region. My task involved working with village and city churches, as well as helping the regional and national Tanzania Assemblies of God. The practical engagement included assisting churches to run conservation agriculture projects in villages such as Kayenze and beekeeping projects in villages such as Ngudu and advising on both a community health education project on Kome Island and an entrepreneurship for social transformation project on Ukerewe Island, all of which are mentioned in this book. And throughout this time I was privileged to teach courses on missiology and biblical studies at St. Paul College, Mwanza, and on practical mission at the church-planting schools, which provided constant challenge and enrichment.

Although my work has been conducted in East Africa – largely Tanzania, some engagement in Kenya and now in Uganda – which serves as the primary context for the book, I believe it has particular applicability to many other places in Africa, especially in sub-Saharan Africa. First, I have engaged with Africans from other countries, both at conferences and through reading, and the same issues and challenges frequently crop up. And second, I have seen that Africans tend to refer to themselves interchangeably as nationals and continentals.

While this book has been written for the African context, several people have brought to my attention that such a book is also needed for the West with many churches struggling to know how to be relevant and make a significant contribution to community transformation in their localities. Their villages, towns, cities and countries are in desperate need of experiencing the light of gospel transformation. Though the issues may differ to a degree from those in Africa, they are no less deep and Western churches are equally called to join with God in community transformation. Western readers should therefore be able to contextualize the approach offered to make it applicable for their situations – something that African students, pastors and theologians have had to do for years when reading books and articles by Western authors.

As African pastors like to say – and I also believe – that "Africa's time is now," my prayer in writing this book is that the double meaning of its title, "Transforming Church," will be displayed in and through the African church so that it will write a rousing new chapter in church history both for the good of Africa and as a stimulus to the rest of the worldwide church.

There are so many people who deserve acknowledgment in the writing of this book. Some are mentioned throughout the pages of the book and it has been my joy to work with them. There are in fact too many to list or even to remember but I know God will not forget them or their labour for his kingdom. I do wish to note Pastor Aldo Maliga, Bishop Charles Mkumbo, Canon Jackson Mwidowe and Pastor Huruma Nkone, godly and servant-hearted pastors with whom I had the privilege of working and who were a constant source of encouragement and wisdom. I also thank my esteemed St. Paul College colleague Marco Methuselah, from whom I learned so much about the African and Sukuma worldviews. Marco kindly read and offered valuable comments on chapter 4. I express my deep appreciation to Bishop Valentine Mbuke for graciously writing the foreword. But more than that, we have enjoyed a rich friendship and working relationship. He exemplifies the type of leadership this book tries to call for and his church, Beacon Mission Christian Centre, is a transforming church. I give my thanks and sincere love to my wonderful Emmanuel International colleagues, without whom none of this work with the church would have been possible. I also thank our many supporters and supporting churches who enabled my family and me to serve God in Africa over the years. I am appreciative to my Amigos Worldwide colleagues in Uganda for the chance to teach through some of the chapters with them and make refinements. I am very grateful to Rachel Lewis who read the entire manuscript and offered insightful contributions to improve it. And I express my thanks to Langham Publishing for kindly publishing this book.

My parents, Edwin and Margaret Monger, who brought me up to know the Lord Jesus and who were able to share in our work in the training of pastors in Tanzania, have my heartfelt gratitude. Though my dad has now died, it is heartening to see his labour in the Lord continuing to bear fruit.

Finally, I wish to thank my family, my wife Rachel and our daughters Amisadai and Louisa, because we could do all this together for the strengthening of the church, the good of Africa and the glory of God. What an adventure it has been!

1

Integral Mission: Will the Church in Africa Take up the Mantle?

God Surprises Us

Amon Suge was the youthful, enthusiastic and hardworking pastor of the Kayenze church, the first church we worked with in the Mwanza region of Tanzania in 2014. His small church of about ten to fifteen members were meeting in a disused cotton storehouse for their weekly gatherings. Kayenze is a fishing village on the shores of Lake Victoria but outside the village centre most inhabitants, including the majority of the church members, are subsistence farmers. The name, Kayenze, derives from the Sukuma word *Mayenze*, meaning "reeds," symbolizing abundance. Villagers say that the strong, vibrant *Mayenze* were located just offshore, but they, along with the abundance the land used to be known for, had sadly long disappeared. Kayenze was symbolic of much of the Mwanza region which was known for its struggle to produce enough food for its population. For this reason, Tanzania Assemblies of God, Mwanza had identified agriculture as one of the opportunities for the church's involvement in community development. Kayenze and its outlying villages were selected as some of the suitable places to begin a conservation agriculture project, not least because Amon was himself a keen farmer.

We conducted the initial classroom training with the small pilot group of farmers, including Amon and his villagers, in which we shared how God was the first farmer, and how the principles of conservation agriculture work out, and then left them the challenge to prepare their fields. Then it was time for us to begin the practical training. My wife and I and our two agriculture trainers, Peter and Esther, turned up full of anticipation to assist Amon in planting on his demonstration farm. Could Kayenze become *Mayenze* once again? Together we followed the principles of conservation agriculture, planting maize and beans, and spreading big piles of rice stems Amon had collected as mulch to cover the soil and aid water retention. Having finished we prayed for God to send the rain, committing the field and the crops to him, knowing that without him there was no chance of success and every chance Amon and his family would go hungry. Kayenze was the Lord's and everything in it (Ps 24).

That year was a good year. Amon helped our trainers to show the other participants how to plant their fields. He also cared for his fields well, weeding them and doing his best to keep his chickens from eating the mulch. He was delighted with the yield from the exhausted soil, harvesting three times as much maize from his conservation agriculture plot as from his conventional agriculture plot. We encouraged him that by continuing with this approach and leaning on God and his wisdom, he could hope for even better harvests in the future as the land healed. And neighbouring villagers, who laughed at us all for smothering the land with grasses on the day we planted, were now also intrigued and asking if they could join the project next year.

In the following years the momentum built, even through times of drought or deluge. More farmers joined the programme each season as they saw or heard of the results. Amon and we conducted further trainings and he loved to impart to others what farming could be like, from both Scripture and experience, when God is involved. He visited participants on their farms, advised them, encouraged them and prayed with them, pastoring those inside and outside the church as they worked. He never tired or lost hope. "God has persevered with us and so we should persevere with others," he encouraged me one day after we experienced frustrations with project participants who seemed not to be participating!

As we worked together in Kayenze, we and our trainers spent considerable time with Amon and the church, often joining the church for worship services. When we were invited, we preached from different angles about the mission God has for us, his church, always seeking to link the agriculture project to that mission. One Sunday, after about four years, it dawned on us what God had done. The church of ten to fifteen members had grown to over a hundred strong. As we talked afterwards, Amon gave thanks for the part the project had played in the increase. "People have become Christians and joined the church through the project," he said. There had been the natural blending of physical and spiritual outcomes. They had seen God's handiwork in creation on the farm, enjoying the subsequent benefits, and had given him praise. This was God's doing. We of course had made many mistakes, some of which I will pick up and address later in the book. But God's blessing and grace and the outworking of his mission were evident. Even today Kayenze is still a work in progress but the signs of God's transforming power are there.

The message I wish to convey in this book is to offer an approach of how the African church can learn in their way to participate more fully with God in his mission in their communities. Not every place will need agriculture like Kayenze. Some places will require water supply, health education, children's ministries, business training, student programmes, advocacy, conflict resolution . . . or more likely a combination of several projects. The setting will vary from remote villages to bustling cities. But in each place, God has work for the church to do, and if we are faithful to work with him, he may surprise us by bringing his transformation through our church to our community. I hope to set out how the pastor, church planter or development worker can help churches to think theologically for themselves and to construct with God's help a culturally appropriate approach to sharing in his all-embracing mission.

The African church has a huge opportunity today to be a blessing to its communities and be part of God's transformation in a way, I believe, no other entity can. Secular organizations see community development as something like *a process where community members come together to identify and take collective action on issues which are important to them* with the aim of increasing quality of life, opportunity, equality and justice. The church can aim higher for thoroughgoing community transformation. (I will consider an apt definition of community development at the end of this chapter.) But although the church is uniquely placed to carry out this transforming role, it has often unfortunately not been able to grasp this place, the reasons for which we will come to later in this chapter. If the oft-quoted saying "The local church is the hope of the world" is to become a reality in its fullest sense, then the church and its servants must be willing to face and address some important opportunities and challenges in today's African contexts. To these we now turn.

The Opportunities the Church Has for Involvement in Community Development

Sometimes the church carries on its life and mission oblivious to the situation around it. In this way, the church acts as if its mission is timeless and fails to be relevant to its context. In one sense, the church's mission is timeless, unchanging. We are still carrying out the same mission Jesus entrusted to his disciples and which they have handed through the generations all the way to us as believers in the twenty-first century. But in another sense, the church's mission is always to be expressed and worked out in ways that respond to the situation of its time, culture and locality, answering the cries of those around. As we will see later, Jesus always responded to the pleas of the poor, needy and oppressed in his vicinity. And the church likewise does best when it is aware of its context and has its eyes and ears open.

So what is the situation which affords the church opportunities in mission and community development? What I offer are just the contours of some of the bigger general opportunities that are commonly understood as relevant and fundamental to much of Africa. There are of course many others, at both continental and local levels, but this brief sketch will suffice for our purposes. I survey the situation in terms of the church's potential response to poverty, the deeper contribution it could make to fill the gaps in relation to the work of non-governmental organizations (NGOs), governments and business, and the church's own growth and increasing capacity.

Poverty

First, although in many ways Africa is a blessed continent, it does face widespread poverty. I will examine the nature of poverty later, but the fact is that wherever we look in Africa we see the poor, in the fields, in the villages, on the streets, in the city centres, even lurking in the wealthy neighbourhoods, desperate for any help they can get. Poverty often exists because of a lack of community development,[1] leading to deprivation and injustice. The church that wants to respond to the poor needs to think long and hard about the nature of poverty and underlying causes in its community, so that it can act like Jesus who, seeing the situation in his time, in launching his radical ministry in the synagogue in Nazareth exclaimed, "The Spirit of the Lord is on me, because he has anointed me to proclaim good news to the poor" (Luke 4:18).

Designing relevant and effective ministries to alleviate poverty is a process for any church. The first stage for the church in seeking to set up such ministries is to understand the general and basic causes of poverty in Africa. After that, the church will need to spend time refining its understanding and considering the more specific reasons for poverty in its locality. For now, I briefly outline some of the basic causes[2] of poverty in Africa as a means of highlighting how

---

1. Without wholesome community development there will be all kinds of deprivation at the personal, family and community levels. There are of course all kinds of external factors that also feed into a community's lack of development, but the point about poverty being caused by a lack of community development still stands.

2. I will sharpen these causes in chapter 4 to include a more holistic treatment but at present the aim is simply to introduce them.

the church, if it has not done so already, can begin to think about its response to poverty. These basic causes include climate change, food insecurity, community health struggles, the lack of education, unemployment, conflict issues, gender disparity and leadership.

Climate change has become a dominant issue of our day in the whole world and not only in Africa. But in Africa, particularly in the rural areas, it is felt acutely.[3] It is often the rural poor who are among the most affected by these changing weather patterns. If anyone doubts climate change is happening, that person should go to rural Africa. Villagers constantly talk about climate change and how it has adversely affected their lives. Hotter temperatures and uneven rainfall are not just inconvenient; they directly affect people who are dependent on the land for their livelihood. Travel too can be made impossible when dirt roads are washed away by flash floods, which can also result in the loss of homes and increase in disease. Although there are global factors in the changing weather patterns in African villages, there are often local factors too. I have seen dramatic variation in weather patterns even within the same region. Some villages have experienced the destruction of the local environment particularly through the excessive cutting down of trees and consequently low rainfall whereas other villages which have managed their forests better enjoy good rainfall. In the towns and cities too it is not uncommon to see the flooding of homes, sewage problems, the loss of life and the knock-on effects to the economy. What can the church which worships the Creator and Sustainer of the universe offer to the ongoing climate change conversation?

Food insecurity is related to climate change but not exclusively. Africans say that previously one could expect one drought year in every ten years but today it is often one in every two or three years. I myself have experienced drought one year and floods the next, neither of which is conducive to good harvests. People also say that years ago they could fairly accurately predict when the rains would come and for how long they would last. But such certainty has long gone. "We just don't know when the rains will come these days," is a common cry. The rains can come early, people plant, and then the rains suddenly stop. But at the same time, bad farming methods and deforestation have also reduced the soil's fertility. And if we consider population growth, the world's population is

---

3. The website 350africa.org highlights the comprehensive way climate change has affected African peoples (see 350Africa.org, "8 Ways Climate Change Is Already Affecting Africa," accessed 29 July 2022, https://350africa.org/8-ways-climate-change-is-already-affecting-africa/).

predicted to increase by 33 percent to 9 billion by 2050.[4] But Africa's population is estimated to double in the same period. So Africa is going to need twice as much food at a time when harvests are declining. Where will the people of God be in facing this issue, especially if they know their story and the occasions when God provided food in drought or desert situations?

Community health is a fundamental issue facing countries in Africa.[5] Issues such as maternal health, malaria, lack of safe water and sanitation, and HIV/AIDS all affect the poor considerably, who then also face added challenges of accessing good healthcare when they become sick. Healthcare facilities are extremely limited and stretched, and good access is available only to those who can afford it. Without good health people cannot work, they cannot provide for themselves and their children, and the cycle of poverty continues. Healthcare is one issue; another is community health education. The poor often lack access to community health education and therefore lack the knowledge about preventable illnesses and diseases. And yet even in the Old Testament there are clear instructions about health practices, including sanitation (Deut 23:12–13).

Education is a universal basic human right but sadly so many children in Africa are denied this right.[6] Such children, many of them extremely bright, grow up and continue the subsistence farming passed down to them or find their way onto the streets. They never get the opportunity to learn and develop and explore new opportunities. It is common to see slogans outside schools such as "Education is life" or "Education is light," but unfortunately many still fail to find life and light. Equally, many teenage girls, having not been taught about how their bodies work, either miss a significant portion of their schooling or give up completely on school once their periods start, due to shame. But throughout church history, the church has always taken a keen interest in education and there is no reason to stop today.

Employment opportunities are often lacking and people are forced to scrape a living doing dead-end, demeaning and unsatisfying work. Every week, in the city, in the village or at my gate, I was asked by young people and old for a

---

4. Saidi Mkomwa in a presentation given at ECHO East Africa Symposium 2015 on Sustainable Agriculture.

5. Seth Selorm Klobodu, Sarah Kessner and Levi Johnson, "Africa Is on the Verge of a Major Health Crisis and the Need for Nutrition and Health Surveys Is Imperative," *The Pan African Medical Journal* 30 (2018): 173, https://www.ncbi.nlm.nih.gov/pmc/articles/PMC6235492/.

6. The United Nations highlights significant challenges in education in Africa (Zipporah Musau, "Africa Grapples with Huge Disparities in Education," *Africa Renewal*, December 2017–March 2018, https://www.un.org/africarenewal/magazine/december-2017-march-2018/africa-grapples-huge-disparities-education).

job. When I enquired what kind of job they were looking for, the reply usually came back, "Anything!" People are desperate for work. This is particularly so among young people, some leaving their homes for the city to "search for life," frequently only to be disappointed.[7] With the lack of work comes hopelessness and despair, confining people to more of the same and with a sense of worthlessness. What a chance for the church and its many successful business people to offer training in entrepreneurship and business skills!

Conflict issues abound in many African countries leaving countless families and communities fearful and destitute, without a home and the means of supporting themselves and their children. Without peace and security these people cannot access basic services, have the ability and confidence to conduct fruitful employment or have hope for their future. But for many people affected by conflict the pain goes much deeper, including the loss of community itself. Conflict issues also occur among settled communities, such as between different tribes or between pastoralists and farmers over land use. I was once asked by a government official to help in resolving conflict because cattle and goat herders were grazing their livestock in others' rice fields. The church has a unique contribution to make among troubled peoples or those torn apart by political unrest because reconciliation lies at the heart of the gospel.[8]

Gender is a hot issue these days and although much has been done to alleviate poverty due to gender inequality there is a long way to go. The World Bank notes, "An African woman faces a 1 in 31 chance of dying from complications due to pregnancy or childbirth, compared to a 1 in 4,300 chance in the developed world."[9] Girls are less likely than boys to have access to education. But studies have shown that if girls can receive a good education, they can make a huge difference to enabling their families to escape poverty. And women still tend to shoulder most of the responsibility in the home and providing for the family but have little influence in decision-making as well as

---

7. Unemployment in Uganda among fifteen- to twenty-five-year-olds is a known concern and one that the Ugandan government tries to hide (Rich Mallett, Teddy Atim and Jimmy Opio, "'Bad Work' and the Challenges of Creating Decent Work for Youth in Northern Uganda," Secure Livelihoods Research Consortium, Briefing Paper 25 [Mar. 2017], https://securelivelihoods.org/wp-content/uploads/%E2%80%98Bad-work%E2%80%99-and-the-challenges-of-creating-decent-work-for-youth-in-northern-Uganda.pdf).

8. The Africa Society of Evangelical Theology devoted an entire volume to this topic (see Rodney L. Reed and David K. Ngaruiya, eds., *Forgiveness, Peacemaking and Reconciliation*, Africa Society of Evangelical Theology Series 5 [Carlisle: Langham Global Library, 2020]).

9. The World Bank, "Improving Gender Equality in Africa," 5 February 2014, https://www.worldbank.org/en/region/afr/brief/improving-gender-equality-in-africa.

being at risk of violence. What contribution could the church, which believes in the equality of all people, make to changing mindsets?

Leadership is another particular issue holding back development and poverty eradication at all levels in Africa, with a lack of honesty, transparency and accountability.[10] Self-seeking and corrupt officials are commonplace, enjoying the power without fulfilling the responsibility to govern and provide the conditions for people to flourish. Money set aside to help community development projects frequently goes missing. We get the advice that if we need permission from an official, we should give them "*kitu kidogo*" (Swahili for "a little something"). However, the church could put forward an alternative leadership style as it follows Jesus, who came "[not] to be served, but to serve" (Mark 10:45).

Plenty of other issues, emerging in urban and rural communities, could be given, but the causes of poverty touched upon above connect with many of the Sustainable Development Goals,[11] which are internationally recognized as foundational for alleviating poverty. So *who* is well placed for tackling poverty? Let us explore this question now.

NGOs

We could ask the question, "Shouldn't we, the church, simply leave the task of tackling such issues to the expert organizations who will be best able to deal with them?" Traditionally, non-governmental organizations (NGOs) have addressed many of these issues and often, if not always, brought change to their beneficiaries. Indeed, there is much to celebrate with the work of many NGOs. They often have dedicated and caring qualified staff who oversee successful poverty-alleviating programmes. I believe that NGOs continue to have a place in community development in Africa and the church would do well to appreciate them and their work and consider partnering with an NGO in certain circumstances (see chapter 7). However, my view is that NGOs are not the only organizations that should be involved in community development, but rather should be among a number of actors to participate in development. And for Christian NGOs, how better to continue than to partner with the

---

10. E.g. Japhace Poncian and Edward S. Mgaya, "Africa's Leadership Challenges in the 21st Century: What Can Leaders Learn from Africa's Pre-Colonial Leadership and Governance?," *International Journal of Social Science Studies* 3, no. 3 (May 2015): 106–15.

11. United Nations, "Do You Know All 17 SDGs?," accessed 29 July 2022, https://sdgs.un.org/goals.

indigenous church (see chapter 5)? But if the work of community development is solely reliant on NGOs, several problems can emerge. The underlying reasons include the following:

Narrow focus of NGOs. Most NGOs focus only on a single issue or a few issues in a restricted field. This is to be expected as an NGO cannot consider everything and would be unsuccessful even if it tried. NGOs have guidelines and particular aims and often cannot step outside these. But there are challenges when we concentrate on only a single issue or have no means of expanding into the next issue. The fact is that our needs are multifaceted and we experience many interrelated issues holding back our development. As an example, when I was working with a church to promote fuel-efficient wood-burning stoves among villagers in an extremely deforested area, together we quickly realized that tree-planting needed to be a key component to bring about greater and lasting benefit. Not to replenish the forests but just to slow the rate of environmental destruction would have been very limited in outlook. It would also have been foolish to train a group of villagers in how to make quality stoves without giving training in business and entrepreneurship. And because the stoves had a health benefit, it naturally led on to training in cooking nutritiously. As we looked at the lack of availability of fresh fruit and vegetables, we then sought to add a gardening dimension to the project. It would be hard to find an NGO that had the agility to address all these areas in a short timescale after beginning the initial project. But because I was working with the church, all these things could be picked up. In fact, after receiving training in entrepreneurship, the group had all kinds of fresh ideas and the team and I were able to support them as they pursued those ideas. If we think about development, we will see that it is about facilitating certain things *leading on* to others. Never just about one issue or a few issues! Or we could think of it as like building a house with a foundation, floors, walls, windows, doors, roofs, furniture and then occupancy, which are all needed in time, but cannot be put in place at the same time. The church has the opportunity to build the whole house as it follows the Architect and calls upon NGOs as specialist tradespeople when necessary. For those working in local or overseas NGOs or missions agencies, I look later at how such work might yield great impact.

Short-term focus of NGOs. As well as a common narrow focus, NGOs frequently have a short-term focus in their development projects, often two to three years. This is because they are usually dependent on funding from other donors or governments. This funding has to be fully spent within the life of the project and there are no guarantees for additional funding later. Donors will expect to see measurable results within the project period. The problem is that it is not that simple. Real and lasting results usually take time and the coordinators cannot control the speed of the take-up of the project. There can be a raft of reasons why the progress does not come as quickly as we had hoped. And sometimes we are just unrealistic or we feel the pressure from donors to expect too much too soon. If the project coordinators can journey with the participants for a longer period, assisting them to overcome the challenges faced and to think through appropriate solutions, the project has a far greater chance of being successful, but few NGOs can afford that kind of luxury of time.

Lack of sustainability in the work of NGOs. Africa is unfortunately littered with good and innovative NGO development projects that suddenly stopped and failed to leave a lasting legacy. Many times, I have visited places to see the sad relics of previous endeavours. This is, to a large degree, the outcome of the previous two points of a narrow and short-term focus, but goes beyond them. Often there is also a lack of thought and planning in how the participants will be able and motivated to continue after the formal duration of the project. It is necessary to ask questions such as: Is this project worth their while in continuing? And what else needs to be introduced so that the project takes off rather than fizzles out? Of course, there can be other factors such as instigating a project in which the coordinators did not listen well to the participants and facilitate their shaping of it. Not all NGOs suffer from a lack of sustainable outcomes through their work, but it must be noted that often the systems NGOs operate under mitigate against achieving a permanent change. By its very nature, development should have lasting results that lead on to other benefits. In the analogy of the house, the foundation, the walls and the roof should remain in place for the occupants to enjoy living in the house for many years. The church is not like an NGO which arrives and leaves after two to three years to move to another place. *The church is resident, sustainable and part of the community.*

Current funding challenges of NGOs. Many NGOs, especially those that rely on funding from the West, are experiencing challenges these days in securing funding.[12] Western countries are experiencing financial difficulties and internal challenges and charities are reporting drops in donations. Bond, the UK network for organizations working in international development, details the nature of the severe challenges that large NGOs are facing, which are only being exacerbated by the COVID-19 pandemic, to the extent that

---

12. The manuscript was essentially written before the recent cost of living rises and the war in Ukraine, which are likely to add pressure to the task of fundraising.

these NGOs may need to reinvent themselves.[13] And smaller NGOs are not immune, with some of their sources drying up, such as through the sudden cuts to USAID and UKAID budgets. This all results in there not being enough money to go around, and it will likely mean that a significant percentage of NGOs will cease to operate in the coming years. But as we will see, the church can operate in a different funding system.

African Governments

We could also ask the question, "Shouldn't we, the church, simply leave the task of tackling issues of community development to the national government as it is their responsibility?" It is indeed the responsibility of the government to care for its citizens, providing education, clean water, healthcare, employment opportunities, transport networks, gender equality, youth training, and so on. It is not my position that the church should take over the responsibilities of a country's national and local government.[14] Rather, the church should be leading the way in holding these governments to account, calling them to do what they promised, insisting on the proper management of the economy for the benefit of all and advocating for the rights of the poor and oppressed. And we can thank God for the wonderful work of advocacy that many Christian organizations are doing. Advocacy work is an intrinsic part of community development where we stand with the poor with the aim that they might gain access to what is rightly theirs as citizens, such as land, opportunities and healthcare. But as well as calling on governments to fulfil their responsibilities, the church has a greater opportunity in community development, sometimes in connection with governments and NGOs, because of at least the following challenges governments face:

Capacity of the government. All governments have limited capacity to fulfil the needs of their citizens and African governments are no exception. There are challenges with the strength of the economies. This is compounded by the debts incurred when richer countries take advantage of others. But the fact is that the ability of the government of an African country to achieve its obligations is curbed, although some are trying to channel more of their own

---

13. Barney Tallack, "5 Existential Funding Challenges for Large INGOs," Bond, 2 July 2020, "https://www.bond.org.uk/news/2020/07/5-existential-funding-challenges-for-large-ingos.

14. The church has of course often set up educational and healthcare institutions which when managed well are good provocations to governments of how to run such institutions effectively.

resources to drive development.[15] It is sadly not uncommon to find district and ward officers charged with a responsibility but having no resources to fulfil it. The church can sometimes work with these officers to enable them to do their work. The needs in many African countries are vast and the budgets are small, so that, for example, 150 students can be crammed into a single classroom with one teacher. How can all the students learn well? District hospitals filled to overflowing with the sick are often staffed by one doctor and two nurses. People thus queue for hours.

Failings of the government. Sadly all governments are fallen and frequently fail their citizens. In Africa this commonly takes the shape of bureaucracy and corruption. To register your business is not a simple process as you are passed from department to department, filling in new forms only to arrive back at the first department. And much aid and development money has poured into African countries only to be misused by government leaders. The issue of leadership highlighted earlier plays right into this problem and even though promises are made at general elections, frequently little seems to change.

Business

"What about business?" Clearly business does have a significant role to play in the development of communities, especially through social enterprises. Sometimes of course business operates out of a different agenda whereby the owners are enriched and unfortunately the poor, who may do much of the work, fail to receive their just deserts. The poor's ability to access equitable loans is often low and they end up at the mercy of those who exploit them.[16] Even though efforts are at work to reform the system, and the goal has to be a greater place for business in achieving lasting development, one can never eradicate human greed. Therefore, the church cannot stand by, expecting business on its own to be an unbridled source of good for the growth of communities. I would urge Christian business owners and entrepreneurs to think through how they can use their God-given talents to begin ethical businesses that transform and/ or pass on their skills to others to run their own businesses.

---

15. It was for instance recognized at Tanzanian president John Magufuli's funeral on 22 March 2021 by other African leaders that he led the way in urging Africa to be less dependent on other nations.

16. E.g. C. S. M. Duggan, "Doing Bad by Doing Good? Theft and Abuse by Lenders in the Microfinance Markets of Uganda," *Studies in Comparative International Development* 51 (2016): 189–208.

If therefore the church leaves the work of community development solely to NGOs, governments and business, the peoples will suffer and the church will largely be seen as irrelevant. Not to be involved in climate change, food security, education, healthcare, creating employment opportunities, gender equality, leadership, and so on, leaves the church with a very minute role indeed.

The Church in Africa

Amid all that has happened, in all that I have outlined above, the church in Africa has been growing, and growing rapidly.[17] This we celebrate: it gives us hope and causes us to thank our God. Since the independence of African states, the leadership of churches in Africa has transferred to indigenous people, and many more churches and denominations have been started. It seems to me that the African church is one of the best examples of sustainability. Not only have the churches survived after independence and the transference to indigenous leadership, but they have thrived. These church and denominational leaders have vision, a vision for the church to grow. Churches are being planted and the vision is maturing. For example, the pan-Africa Assemblies of God Alliance has integral mission (defined later) as one of its three main emphases. A few years ago, one would have expected a vision with a focus just on the Holy Spirit and spiritual mission, but things are changing. So with the church in Africa growing as a significant force, and the limitations of NGOs, governments and business to alleviate poverty and bring lasting transformation, can the church grasp the opportunity to share more widely in community development as an integral part of its overall mission? As the church ponders this, it will be wise to consider, where possible and appropriate, how to connect with the contributions of NGOs, government and business for a symbiotic relationship.[18] And those in Christian agencies can think of working through the local church for deeper poverty alleviation and greater impact.

---

17. Missiologist Michael Goheen notes the growth in Christianity in sub-Saharan Africa from less than 10 percent of the population in 1900 to around 60 percent in 2014 (Michael W. Goheen, *Introducing Christian Mission Today: Scripture, History and Issues* [Downers Grove: IVP Academic, 2014], 191).

18. This symbiosis is recognized by Peter Greer and Chris Horst of Hope International in their book *Mission Drift: The Unspoken Crisis Facing Leaders, Charities and Churches* (Minneapolis: Bethany House, 2014), 174.

The Challenges the Church Must Face Honestly

In any part of life, if we are to grasp the opportunities that come to us, it behoves us to be willing and able to face the ensuing obstacles. The student who wins a scholarship to a top university must be willing to knuckle down to do the hard work if the opportunity is not to be wasted. In this section I wish to identify some of the key challenges the church must overcome if it is to be significantly involved in community development. I shall group these under the headings "Resetting the vision" and "The need for contextualization."

Resetting the Vision

Although the African church is growing and developing, what kind of vision does it have? And what kind of vision does it require if genuine community development, whereby poor communities are lifted up, is to have a significant place in the life and ministry of the church? These are the questions I explore in this section, which I believe the African church must address if it is to be a key player in healthy development.

A whole vision. Vision is a big challenge, and while many African churches have a large vision – larger often than the vision of their Western counterparts – it is not always clear what place community development has in that vision. Often there is a lack of cohesive vision in which all of the parts contribute towards a unified whole. Many churches can have departments – worship, discipleship, men's ministry, women's ministry, youth and children's ministry, evangelism, mission, development, education – which all tend to take on a life of their own without necessarily talking to one another. The problem is that mission and development relate to men, women, youth, children and so on. It is usually especially unhelpful when there are separate mission and development departments. What tends to happen then is that the mission department concentrates on spiritual matters, bringing people to Christ, and the development department attends to physical matters, bringing people clean water and healthcare. Both these departments therefore get pulled out of shape and church members can be confused as to what is really important to the church as there appears to be a split-up vision.

A wholesome vision. As well as a whole vision, the church needs a wholesome vision. If the church wants to be used powerfully by God in participating in his mission, then it needs to deal with issues such as prosperity, corruption, politics and syncretism. The prosperity gospel has made tremendous inroads in the church in Africa and it stands at odds with the true gospel, the gospel of the cross. The prosperity gospel centres in the love of self, on what I can get by following God in terms of personal success and wealth. To do good community development we need to embrace the true gospel which centres in God and his agenda, involving the love of God and neighbour. In the same way, the church must be open and deal with the corruption in its midst. This includes church officials in their church responsibilities and church members in their conduct and work. Eighty percent of the population of Kenya purports to be Christian and yet corruption abounds. When I conversed with a Kenyan pastor about this issue, he replied honestly, "We need to take 80 percent of the responsibility." As mentioned above, love of neighbour is paramount to good community development, as we are motivated, not by our greed or the greed of others, but by the good of the poor, who have been badly served by corrupt systems. Church politics are also harmful to community development since wrong agendas come to the fore, decisions are made for the powerful, and the church and its God-given vision get sidelined. Syncretism, the mixing of Christian faith with other religious elements against it (e.g. animism and witchcraft), contaminates and weakens the wholesome vision of transformation God has for his church. None of these issues is unique to the African church, but the church in Africa must be honest in dealing with and eradicating how these issues express themselves in its context.

A vision wholly set on God. One of the things I love about Africa is the oft-quoted expression "God is able." And indeed he is! But when one explores the possibility of the church involving itself in community development, in reaching out practically to the poor, the frequent reply is, "We can't because we don't have money." While there are lots of reasons why this view has arisen, not least because people have seen Western money flowing in to aid development (not always successfully, I may add), there is good reason to challenge it. Why did Jesus send the disciples out on mission telling them not to take money (Mark 6:6–13 and par.)? Because he had given them everything they needed. When our eyes are firmly on God and our ears attentive to the Holy Spirit, we have confidence in God to supply all we need, for it is his work anyway, and we need not allow what we lack to cause us to make excuses. As stated above, the church can operate in a different funding system. We should realize, as Hudson Taylor, missionary to China, said long ago, "God's work, done in God's way, will never lack God's supply." This relates to human resources, finances, wisdom, energy, the Holy Spirit and all the other resources we need to carry out God's work. I can honestly say that in all my time in Africa I have never failed to start or had to stop a project through a lack of resources. God is extremely faithful. But we must keep this whole saying in mind. Churches may and often do see a lack of supply for community development projects either because the projects are not really part of God's work or more commonly because the projects are not being done in God's way due to other, selfish or corrupt church agendas. If, however, the church and the church leadership is captured fully by the vision of God's mission and sets its community development within that mission (chapters 2 and 3), then it can believe God to supply all its needs to bless others. I will look at this issue of funding further in chapters 5 and 7 in which we will see that it is important for the church, having placed its confidence in God, to *own* the funding issue for the work to become sustainable.

The Need for Contextualization

It may sound obvious and silly to say but Uganda is not the UK and Tanzania is not America. Uganda is Uganda and Tanzania is Tanzania. What works in the UK does not work in Uganda and what works in America does not work in Tanzania. Many projects in Africa fail to achieve the desired results because they operate through Western frameworks. We must acknowledge there is much to be commended about a Western mindset which can have some useful elements for development in Africa, but it also possesses unhelpful elements. At this stage, it is important to mention that this challenge of contextualization needs to be acknowledged openly, rather than remaining latent, since otherwise disappointment and hurt can be felt later.

The challenge of contextualization happens on at least a couple of fronts: first, through the Western partners that may work with the African church, and second, through globalization more generally and the type of training that many key Christian leaders in Africa receive.

The challenges with Western partners. Western practitioners in community development, although frequently being well qualified, tend to come with uncritical Western attitudes and values. They may be unaware of some of these but nonetheless often do not take the time to humble themselves, learn the local culture and dialogue with project participants to sufficiently understand the situation on the ground. There can be an attitude that they know what is best and they design the project themselves. If they have sourced the funding, there can be a sense that the project is theirs to run. They can also be captive to their ideals rather than to the needs and opportunities of the local people. They often see poverty only in material terms, reflecting Western outlooks on materialism and consumerism, rather than seeing poverty more holistically. And if they are Christian, they then can bring their Western theology and presuppositions leading to, for example, an individualized response or a one-sided view of the atonement. Furthermore, many of the resources on development have been written by those with a Western outlook.[19] African churches, if they have Western partners, may unbeknown to themselves fall prey to Western agendas which have been written into project proposals. Donors can be very insistent on what they want, such as the preference for "measurable" (and sometimes, to be honest, superficial) data.

The challenges of globalization and "Western" training. The African church is not an island but is situated within the worldwide Christian family as well as being exposed to the global trends of the day, many of which originate from fallen Western culture. African churches need to be aware of how much Western thought they themselves have imbibed. Many educated bishops and pastors received their training in the West or with Western theology. In the Bible college where I taught in Tanzania, although I was the only non-African, almost all the books in the library were written by UK, Canadian or US authors, who naturally tend to write with their contexts in mind. The lack of contextualization has done a lot of damage to community development efforts. Although much progress in this area has occurred, greater efforts to a more contextualized response are desperately needed. There are helpful resources to thinking about the Western mindset and its effect on community projects, such as the insightful book *When Helping Hurts.*[20] But that book is written mainly for an American or Western audience. What is needed is a thoroughgoing African treatment. The present book seeks to take steps towards this aim by attempting to critically appraise Western and African cultures in the light of the Bible and arrive at an approach suitable for the lasting development of particular local communities (see chapter 4).[21]

Transforming Church

We have seen a huge open door for the growing church in Africa to embrace more fully a more extensive mission and involve itself in community development among the poor. My prayer is that the church in Africa will increasingly take up this mantle by embracing integral mission as the mission God has called it to. I believe the church can offer communities a better transformation than that offered by NGOs, governments and businesses, because the church

---

19. This present book is an attempt to take the African context seriously.

20. Steve Corbett and Brian Fikkert, *When Helping Hurts: How to Alleviate Poverty without Hurting the Poor . . . and Yourself*, 2nd ed. (Chicago: Moody, 2012).

21. I like to encourage African students studying in the West to go with the mindset of seeing how their African perspectives can infuse life into Western churches and bring renewal.

has, as we will see in the next two chapters, *a better narrative*, holding out the opportunity through Christ and by the Spirit of real, deep and lasting personal and communal renewal.[22] To make its efforts most transformative, the church will do well to draw on – and rework within its narrative – the wise contributions of NGOs, governments and businesses, and where possible and appropriate build relationships with these other actors. For those who work in Christian NGOs and agencies, there is the chance to partner with the church so it enters through that huge open door.

David Bosch, the South African missiologist, wrote a seminal book thirty years ago entitled *Transforming Mission*[23] in which he detailed the exciting shifts taking place in mission.[24] These shifts have continued and others happened too. But if mission is to be both transformed and transforming, then the church needs to be both transformed and transforming; hence the title of this book, *Transforming Church*. I look at how the church in Africa can work towards this, first by seeing the breathtaking all-encompassing vision of God's story of mission and the place of the church in that mission which includes community development (chapters 2–3). Second, I look at working with the church conceptually and theologically (chapters 4–6), and third, I describe working out that theological vision practically (chapters 7–9). The aim is to see our practice faithfully expressing what we believe. I offer a final encouragement to the church by using John's gospel to reflect on the way Jesus lives out his mission and how he sets up his followers to continue this mission (chapter 10).

Before doing so, I should define what I mean by the terms *integral mission* and *community development*. These of course mean different things to different people. Integral mission is sometimes known as "holistic mission," rightly emphasizing the whole-life nature of mission as opposed to simply trying to save souls. It thus recognizes that nothing is outside God's redeeming and transforming mission. Some argue, though, that "integral mission" is a better and more humble term, since it emphasizes through witness and service God's

---

22. Bryant Myers details research that shows situations where Pentecostal churches have been more effective in community development than NGOs (Bryant L. Myers, "Progressive Pentecostalism, Development, and Christian Development NGOs: A Challenge and an Opportunity," *International Bulletin of Missionary Research* 39, no. 3 [Jul. 2015]: 115–20).

23. David J. Bosch, *Transforming Mission: Paradigm Shifts in Theology of Mission* (Maryknoll: Orbis, 1991).

24. These are (1) mission as the church-with-others, (2) mission as *missio Dei*, (3) mission as mediating salvation, (4) mission as the quest for justice, (5) mission as evangelism, (6) mission as contextualization, (7) mission as liberation, (8) mission as inculturation, (9) mission as common witness, (10) mission as ministry by the whole people of God, (11) mission as witness to people of other living faiths, (12) mission as theology and (13) mission as action in hope.

greater and whole reality.[25] Often debated is whether the gospel encompasses both evangelism and social action and, if so, which has priority, or whether there are social and for that matter other consequences of the gospel.[26] To me, this is a largely unhelpful and Western debate, since clearly God's mission is comprehensive (but see chapter 6). The Micah Declaration helpfully uses "integral mission" to mean "the proclamation and demonstration of the gospel,"[27] a mission that involves being, doing and telling in unison. While agreeing with this I would also add that *integral mission seeks through the gospel to integrate into a healthy relationship what sin has damaged and broken apart but what God always intended should be together for human flourishing* (e.g. persons, families, communities, work and the rest of creation). Integral mission works towards full transformation and believes in the lordship of Christ over everything. Every part of the mission, whether spiritual, physical, social, economic or environmental, has value. Integral mission understands that God is the Creator and the Reconciler of all things.

The concept of community development originated in secular thinking to mean something like "a process where community members are supported by agencies to identify and take collective action on issues which are important to them."[28] I would modify this to say it is *the church working with the community to see the community developing as God intends, thus enjoying his goodness and living increasingly under the lordship of Jesus Christ: personally, socially, physically, spiritually, economically and environmentally.* This kind of community development is thus intrinsically linked to integral mission, being both the outworking and the outcome of such mission. Throughout the book, I will continue to use these two intersecting terms, *integral mission* and *community development*, often together in the same sentence, to help the reader keep in mind the full picture of this part of the church's mission – its shape and outcome. To put flesh on these bones and see what God's vision is

---

25. Charles Ringma, "Holistic Ministry and Mission: A Call for Reconceptualization," *Missiology: An International Review* 32, no. 4 (Oct. 2004): 431–48.

26. See Jamie A. Grant and Dewi A. Hughes, *Transforming the World? The Gospel and Social Responsibility* (Nottingham: Apollos, 2009). For an understanding of how the term "integral mission" came into being, see C. René Padilla, "Integral Mission and Its Historical Development," in *Justice, Mercy and Humility: Integral Mission and the Poor*, ed. Tim Chester (Carlisle: Paternoster, 2002), 42–58.

27. Quoted from Tim Chester, "Introducing Integral Mission," in Chester, *Justice, Mercy and Humility*, 1–11.

28. Jessica Smart, "What Is Community Development?," Australian Institute of Family Studies (AIFS), updated 2019, https://aifs.gov.au/resources/practice-guides/what-community-development.

for communities and how we can participate with him in taking steps towards realizing this vision, let us now turn to the Bible. In this way, we will gain our foundational understanding of mission and community development.

2

Community Development within the Overarching Story of God's Mission (Part 1)

Introduction

When it comes to wholesome community development there is no better foundational resource than the Bible! Its impact throughout history of bringing transformation is there to be seen, such as in its shaping of rights for all humans.[1] For Christians, this is because the Bible is God's word and in it God has revealed his ways for human communities to flourish. It is therefore sensible in contemplating how the church in Africa can grasp the opportunities for mission and community development to look first at the *biblical vision of thriving communities enjoying God and his goodness and the mission of the people of God in seeing this vision come to fruition.* But before moving into the Bible, we should ask, "What kind of book is it?"

The Bible as Story

When teaching missiology in Tanzania, I have always enjoyed asking my students on the first day of class where mission begins in the Bible. What is fascinating is how, in the discussion that follows, the views offered move progressively earlier in the Bible: Acts 2, Matthew 28, Genesis 12, Genesis 3:15.

---

1. Lauren Green McAffee and Michael McAfee, "The Bible's Impact on Human Rights," *Christianity Today* online, 28 June 2019, https://www.christianitytoday.com/ct/2019/june-web-only/not-what-you-think-michael-lauren-mcafee.html.

On one occasion one student, Emmanuel, finally suggested, "I think mission in the Bible began when God created the world."

One of the great advances in biblical studies over recent years is the fresh recognition that the Bible is *narrative* in shape. The Bible is story. It is not fundamentally a textbook or rule book to be dipped into, but a story designed to be read as one book from cover to cover. And as we read the Bible, we come to know the Author and his work and are offered the chance to participate with him. There is tremendous power in story: stories shape your view of reality and invite you to live within a different narrative.[2] Africans are story-based people,[3] with their stories being told from generation to generation. Every community, tribe and nation has stories which give its people meaning, identity, values, beliefs and a way of being in the world. But all of our own stories are broken and incomplete, and hence so are we (see chapter 4).

The Bible is *God's* story, the *true* story of the world, and God invites us into it, healing and fulfilling our broken stories. He calls us to live his story! As we turn to the Bible, we find the whole Bible is the *story* of God's mission or *missio Dei*.[4] Emmanuel, my student, was right: mission does begin in Genesis 1, and moreover continues through tough times right to Revelation 22. As we will see, *story* is the key idea that unlocks God's mission to us, which is weaved throughout the Bible. Stories have a beginning, plot, conflict, resolution, characters . . . and so does the Bible! And what is more, as we become reconciled to God through Jesus, we become characters in his story with our part to play in his mission. Our role in God's mission is about opening the true story to people and inviting them in.

The "chapters" or "acts" of the story of the Bible can be laid out as follows:

Creation

Crisis

Calling of Abraham and Israel

Christ

Church

Consummation

---

2. A wonderful example of this is Jesus's retelling of Israel's story to the two on the road to Emmaus and correcting their perception of it, such that they were changed and renewed (Luke 24:13–35).

3. Because of this, a narrative approach to the Bible connects well with Africans (see Joseph Healey and Donald Sybertz, *Towards an African Narrative Theology* [Maryknoll, NY: Orbis, 1996]).

4. *Missio Dei* is a Latin phrase meaning "the mission of God."

In this chapter and the next, I will outline God's great story, drawing out insights for integral mission and community development for Africa and summing these up at the end of each "act." *The aim is that we will be shaped by God's view of reality, his powerful story, so that we do not inadvertently offer communities our broken, incomplete and ineffectual stories.*

I. Creation and Community Development
The Creation of the World: Genesis 1:1 – 2:3

When we look at the creation account (Gen 1–2), we see God's design of the world, his intention for human beings and their role in the world. The opening sentence, "In the beginning God created the heavens and the earth" (1:1), likely summarizes the whole account (1:1 – 2:3), showing that what follows is *all God's doing*. A right understanding of the word "to create" (*bara*) is essential for our purposes. Old Testament scholar John Walton argues that the intent of *bara* is not so much the making without materials as the bringing of heaven and earth into operational existence by "assigning roles and functions," and therefore a possible English word to use is "to design."[5] Verse 2 begins the account proper, describing the negative state of the earth before creation as "formless and empty" (Heb. *tōhû wābōhû*), meaning "unproductive emptiness." Sadly today, many communities in Africa, through painful events or injustice, display indications of being formless and empty, lacking organization and signs of life. But what follows should give every African hope! We are expectant for something to burst forth, as we see "the Spirit of God . . . hovering over the waters" (v. 2).

The actual creation account has a distinct overall structure (1:3–31):

Form (in response to *tōhû*)	Fill (in response to *bōhû*)
1. Light (vv. 3–5)	4. Lights (vv. 14–19)
Day	Greater light (sun)
Night	Lesser light (moon)
2. Firmament (vv. 6–8)	5. Inhabitants (vv. 20–23)
Sky	Birds
Waters	Fish
3. Dry land (vv. 9–13)	6. Land animals / Humanity (vv. 24–31)
Vegetation	
Seed-bearing plants	

---

5. John H. Walton, *Genesis*, NIV Application Commentary (Grand Rapids, MI: Zondervan, 2001), Kindle loc. 1380.

In verse 3, God begins his work of creation by *forming* (Days 1–3) and *filling* (Days 4–6), in response to the *formlessness* and *emptiness* he found at the beginning. By forming, God shapes and rules over creation before then filling it with *life*. On Day 1 (vv. 3–5), God creates light and then separates the light from the darkness, thus creating *time*. Day 2 (vv. 6–8) shows God making a dome or firmament, which we call "sky," to separate the waters above from the waters below, designing a functional *weather system*.[6] On Day 3 (vv. 9–13), there are two acts of creation: (1) the gathering of the earthly waters to create dry "land" and "seas," and (2) the production of vegetation – various seed-bearing plants and trees (including fruit trees). God has thus created the conditions for *agriculture* which needs soil and water sources and the reproduction of plants.

On the fourth day (vv. 14–19), God creates the sun and the moon to serve as lights in the dome to rule the day and night and to give light to the earth. These two lights serve to mark seasons, days and years. In many other ancient (and modern) cultures the sun, moon and stars were deities, but here they are created and designated to carry out God's purpose. On Day 5 (vv. 20–23), God creates the water creatures to fill the waters and the birds to fill the sky/ heavens. He blesses them (the first blessing), empowering them to be creative and extend life into the uninhabited places.

Finally, on Day 6 (vv. 24–31), God undertakes two acts of creation of creatures to fill the land and enjoy the vegetation of Day 3: land animals and human beings. In verse 26, creation builds to a crescendo with God's words, "Let us make mankind in our image." This is a stunning introduction to human beings and means *we all* have been made to be and act like God, possess his life and represent him.[7]

But then God expands this by blessing (i.e. empowering) us to fulfil our role: "Be fruitful and increase in number; *fill* the earth and subdue it. *Rule* over the fish in the sea and the birds in the sky and over every living creature that moves on the ground" (v. 28, emphasis added). Here we see the role of humanity in creation: we too are to rule and fill. *We are drawn into God's own work of forming and filling*, participating in the *missio Dei*. Human beings are

---

6. See Bill T. Arnold, *Genesis*, NCBC (New York: CUP, 2008), 41, for how this was understood in the ancient Near East.

7. Cf. Gen 2:7; Hab 2:19; Jer 10:14. Furthermore, the king was seen as the carrier of the divine spirit and so his words and acts were understood as expressions of the god living in him (D. J. A. Clines, "The Image of God in Man," *Tyndale Bulletin* 19 [1968]: 53–103). And as verses 26–27 show, this is true of *all* human beings, male and female alike, and not just the king as in other ancient Near Eastern parallels.

designed to function as God's image-bearers to rule over the rest of creation, carrying forth his purpose, often referred to as the *Creation Mandate*. God's purpose in creation involves us as regents of creation so that all creation might flourish as he intends. This ruling relates to all that is in creation – the spheres of people, communities, education, business, science, the arts, land management, beekeeping, forestry, animal husbandry . . . and how these spheres interconnect. So we see what rulership looks like: lovingly directing and providing the conditions for life.

The climax of creation is reached on Day 7 (2:2–3) with the sanctification of the Sabbath day. God has ordered everything in his realm by his word and he rules as King in Sabbath rest over his creation, which is filled with his very presence. And he gives us the gift of the Sabbath that we might also share in the rest of our King and so confess his lordship and our consecration to him.

Insights gained from other ancient Near Eastern (ANE) creation accounts suggest that in Genesis 1 God is constructing the world as his scintillating cosmic *temple-kingdom*.[8] God acts as King by ordering into being and naming everything in creation, and then ruling over it in Sabbath rest. His intent is that everything in creation will reflect his will as an expression of his kingship. The Spirit is often seen in the Bible as playing a role in building the tabernacle or temple (cf. Exod 31:1–11). Here the Spirit is hovering over the surface of the deep, being portrayed as the architect of God's cosmic temple. The mention of the sun and moon as "lights" may be referring to the lamps used in the tabernacle.[9] And on the sixth day, God places humanity as his image in his temple. The world, therefore, is designed to reflect God's kingship and his glory, and our *role* as human beings is to participate in seeing this temple-kingdom grow. The question is, how will this play out?

The Garden of Eden: Genesis 2:4–25

As we read on in the story, we see Genesis 2 contains another account of creation, not in competition with Genesis 1 but from a different angle. Genesis 1 was God-centred, with God initiating, God being sovereign, but with humanity as the pinnacle of creation, and this sets the context for Genesis 2 where the

---

8. Sometimes referred to as *palace-temple* (see Rikk Watts, "Making Sense of Genesis 1," *Stimulus* 12, no. 4 [Nov. 2004]: 2–12). While these other ANE parallels do not possess the authority of the Bible, they can be immensely useful in appreciating the general context in which the biblical authors wrote.

9. So Walton, *Genesis*, Kindle loc. 2674.

perspective now shifts to our *role* in the world. We see this pinnacle and how it is to work with a zoom lens.

First, there is the setting in which we see the unproductive state of the earth at the beginning (vv. 5–6). There are no plants or rain, just streams going anywhere (probably subsurface waters not being utilized for irrigation). And most of all, there is no person to work and cultivate the land and bring about God's intention for creation (cf. 1:28).

Next, we see God beginning to rectify the situation, with the creation of a human being (v. 7). He *forms* the man from "the dust of the ground" (like a potter forming clay) and then *fills* the man with his own breath. The Hebrew words for "man" and "ground" are respectively the related words *ādām* and *ădāmâ*. By being made from dust, soil or ground, we are fashioned with a body suitable for an earthly existence. As human beings, we have a relationship with the earth which is vital for our and creation's flourishing. But more than that, at the same time, we see the emphasis on the holiness of human life; God is forming us as his images and breathes his life into us. We have been made for an earthly existence *with God.*

Then, in the middle of the earth, God plants "the garden of Eden," meaning "protected paradise," and places the man in it (vv. 8–9, 19–20). Here we see something more of *God's design* for the world with an array of people, animals, birds, fish and birds enjoying harmoniously the lush space of crops, trees and winding rivers. Creation is set up to be sustainable, with a system of permaculture and agroforestry with various seed-bearing plants and trees (2:9; cf. 1:11–13),[10] all served by a river in its midst. We see that the garden is abundant, with many life forms together. There is peace and harmony (with no naughty monkeys pinching the maize and bananas); there is biodiversity, there is interdependency, there is a balance.

What do we notice about the role of human beings (2:15)? It is to cultivate *and* take care of the garden. Together these tasks emphasize two vital components of community development. Interestingly, the Hebrew words (*ʿābad* and *šāmar*) for these two functions, which are translated as "to work/ serve" and "to keep, watch or protect," are later used of the work of the priests in the temple (Num 3:7–10). If African communities saw their work in priestly terms, what would the difference be?

God gives the man a command, a test to see if he will live by God's revelation and not by sight, accepting that God knows what is best for him

---

10. In the Bible trees are often seen as a symbol of life (cf. Ps 1:3; Jer 17:6) and are an essential part of the farming system (e.g. Ezek 34:27).

(2:16–17). He then enables the man with community (vv. 18–25). Although the thrust of the passage is on the LORD God's providing a wife for the man and the two entering into true oneness of relationship, this comes in the context of the work of the garden whereby the wife is given as a helper.[11] Equally, while the passage focuses on the husband-and-wife relationship, an important principle is laid down; namely, of the need for *community* (v. 18). This means we were made for community, which includes pulling together as a whole and offering our gifts and strengths to the community and receiving theirs. Dan Fountain provides an apt summary of these verses:

> God provides what we need to take care of the land he has given us. This includes good minds to think, to study, and the knowledge we need to care for the land. We have strong bodies to work hard. He has given us families, friends and communities. We must work hard to care for what God has made and given to us.[12]

Before leaving this passage, we should stand back and ask, "Does God care only about the garden?" Although some Christians would answer, "Yes," this passage cries out, "No!" Outside the garden of Eden there is a vast desert, both a spiritual and a physical desert (2:5–6). God puts a *seed of hope* for the world in this garden. He cares for the whole world, because a river flows from Eden into the world (vv. 10–14)! From Eden the river divides into four and goes in four directions. Here the garden is a *temple-garden* and mediates the abundant supply of heavenly life to the four corners of the earth.[13] God's intention is for all creation to be filled with his life. What is apparent is that God wants the boundaries of the garden to be extended outwards.[14] If the river of God's blessing reaches the desert and brings life, the desert will become part of the

---

11. The word "helper" challenges African cultures on a couple of fronts. First, the woman is given as a helper, not as a slave! The thrust is on husbands and wives sharing the responsibility, especially if people are to see the full blessing of God in their work. Second, the word "helper" does not imply having a lower capacity. We get help with the work we cannot manage on our own. Someone adds strength to what we are lacking. This is in keeping with the Old Testament usage, where "helper" is frequently used of God himself, as in "God is my helper," and he cannot be viewed as the weaker one with lower capacity.

12. Dan Fountain, ed., *Let's Restore Our Land* (Fort Myers: Echo, 2007), 5.

13. See Bruce K. Waltke, *Genesis: A Commentary* (Grand Rapids,: Zondervan, 2001), 87. Gardens were often associated with temples in the ancient world. Temples had a function of disseminating life to the people and the land. Here Adam is likened to a priest with the commands given to him in v. 15. This therefore begins the biblical theme of *temple* which is supposed to be the joining of heaven and earth, whereby heaven's life flows out into the world (cf. Ezek 47:1–12; Rev 22:1–5).

14. There are "gold," "resin" and "onyx," rich resources outside the garden for us to use to fulfil our calling (Gen 2:11–12). God clearly desires we do not simply remain inside the garden.

garden and the boundaries of the garden will be pushed out. Since Genesis 1 precedes Genesis 2 and sets the context for it, this story cannot be simply about a small flourishing garden, but is rather about how God's intention for the whole earth to be ruled and filled with his life comes to fruition (1:28). This interprets humanity's "ruling" (1:28) to include a priestly stewardship of creation.

Contribution to Community Development

Genesis 1–2 is foundational to our understanding of God's intentions for humanity and for how healthy development takes place within communities. I highlight four themes:

The community's vital connection to the God of the world. Genesis 1 presents God as the God, all-powerful, and solely responsible for all creation. He is seen without beginning, without opposition and without limitation, who creates by word, building this marvellously ordered and life-filled world, as his *temple-kingdom*, where he is to be worshipped and obeyed by all. In African thinking there is usually the idea of a Supreme Being. And while there are many similarities between this being and the God of the Bible, as Elizabeth Mburu says, "the God of the Bible is clearly superior."[15] In many African cultures the Supreme Being is seen as distant, whereas the God of the Bible, although distinct from creation, is committed to it and involved. In the opening chapters of Genesis we see God himself "walking" in his creation, desiring close fellowship with us, the people he has made. The world God has made is one of harmony and wholeness and he himself is the One who sustains the world. Churches should help communities come into a good understanding of who God is, ousting unhelpful aspects traditionally handed down to them, so as to discover that they come into order and life *through him*, rather than through ancestors or spirits.

Genesis 2 reveals the necessity of a vital connection to this God for good community development to occur, both within and extending the bounds of "the garden." This is where secular approaches to African development often fall down. The work to uphold and invigorate communities is priestly work, which depends on prayer, mediating God's full life to others, and accepting that his design is best (cf. 2:16–17).

Human beings: image of God and rulership. It is intriguing that Genesis 1 links our identity as image-bearers to our God-given task. By being made in

---

15. Elizabeth Mburu, *African Hermeneutics* (Carlisle: HippoBooks, 2019), 37.

God's image, we can act like God and reveal his goodness to the rest of creation so that it experiences his blessing. God plants crops, flowers and trees, and so should we. God made a beautiful and fruitful garden, and so should we. God rules over creation caringly, and so should we. People need to reflect on the depth, value and significance of who God has created them to be. This is particularly significant given that the identity of many African peoples was supressed through colonialism, but Genesis 1 sets forth their true identity. It is time for people to put this awesome identity to work in their communities. We should recognize that God has assigned to us the task of ruling and filling in our part of creation, and not leave it to others. Our role as humans, as God's vice-regents, is to see this world grow and develop as God's kingdom – ordered, whole and abundant. Our mission is comprehensive in that God's own kingship over all things is to be seen and extended. We must be concerned with the responsible development of community and the environment because God has set these up to be interdependent. But I note that, in contrast to much community development today, God's work here is people-centred rather than environment-focused, since only people are made in his image. We see that we are central to God's plan for the world, and not an afterthought. There is here a particular role of the local church to act as priests towards the community, mobilizing and opening the community to God's vision of transformation.

Communities' requirement of a carefully interconnected design to flourish. We see God's careful design of the world, bringing necessary elements into play stage by stage, so that everything exists in a symbiotic relationship.[16] First, he takes his time to make an environment and world suitable for humanity, the pinnacle of his work, before placing them in position to rule over that world and extend his blessing into every locality. Likewise, the work of community development requires careful attention, planning and design, using God's whole vision of a thriving unified creation, rather than just picking up one or two issues (e.g. gender empowerment or community health). Of course, communities cannot do everything at once but must prioritize, so long as they realize that these are the first and not the only things to do. But communities must be motivated by an interconnected vision of development encompassing whole people, healthy relationships, home life, work, opportunity and environment which together display the glory of God who is to be praised by all. And as they work towards this, they should be mindful to form and to fill. To use an example from agriculture, we often need to begin in our fields by

---

16. E.g. birds and fish are significant for the ecosystem, including for pollinating seeds and recycling nutrients in waters.

subduing the weeds, ruling them before they rule our fields, and only then do we prepare the soil and plant our crops to *fill* the land with life. Furthermore, six times we see God evaluating his work, noting that it was good (1:10, 12, 18, 21, 25 and 31), and communities need to be monitoring and evaluating their development to ensure it fits the agreed design. And Sabbath is part of this design where communities worship their Creator who rules over all things and commit themselves to serving him and his agenda.

Working as a community. Genesis 2 (and Genesis 3 by contrast!) shows that success happens in community as the community is mobilized to work harmoniously together for the common good. First, the community can come together and decide collectively what to do and assign roles. And second, those who are succeeding can make themselves available to those who are struggling. For example, those who have skills in agriculture and animal husbandry, enjoying integrated abundant farms with the garden of Eden as their vision, can use these skills to reach out to others both as a model for others and to assist the poor (e.g. widows, people with disabilities and those with HIV/AIDS) to farm well to bring transformation in their lives. In this way, the boundaries of the desert will be pushed further back and people may then come to know their Creator and give praise to the One who has supplied their needs.

As communities work together, they must remember the two tasks given in the garden: "cultivation" and "taking care/keeping." The first emphasizes developing and progressing, and the second maintaining what has been achieved. Many projects in Africa have concentrated on the first task but ignored the second, resulting in no lasting impact. This second responsibility includes protecting what has been achieved and driving the "enemies" far from the community, like the serpent who is about to appear. We can think about this second responsibility of caring for creation in larger terms too, such as putting in place integrated systems which properly manage soil, land and water resources, for us and our neighbours but also for our children and children's children after us.

In drawing this section to a close, we see this gives the church a huge mandate to be involved in community development as an essential and integral part of its mission, which is to see God's kingdom and temple fill the earth, where he is personally present. Otherwise, the church limits its relevance and hands over such responsibility to others, to the detriment of all. The first two chapters of the Bible have already shown the Bible's relevance to the basic causes of poverty identified in chapter 1: those of climate change, food insecurity, community health struggles, the lack of education, unemployment, conflict issues, gender disparity and leadership.

God's creating of the world is the foundation for the biblical story: as it meanders and progresses, the story looks forward to the redemption, healing and transformation of all creation. May there be signs through the church of these *today* in family and intertribal relationships, farming, beekeeping, tree-planting, education, science, the arts, business and politics, whereby the blessing of God is released in every sphere and flows from one sphere into another, bringing a synergy of life and renewal.

II. Crisis: The Fall and Community (Un)Development
The World Falls Apart: Genesis 3

Sadly, we know what happens and those delightful chapters we hoped for following Genesis 2 never get written. Instead, there is rebellion in the kingdom and against the King. The man and the woman disobey God, having been deceived by the crafty serpent, who promised that eating the fruit of the tree would open their eyes to a whole new world (Gen 3:5). They ate the fruit and "the eyes of both of them were opened," but not to what they expected, for "they realised that they were naked; so they sewed fig leaves together and made coverings for themselves" (3:7). They had been duped; not all that glitters is gold. And there is no going back! The consequences are terrible – the wheels come off everything! All creation feels the weight of God's judgement.

There is judgement against the serpent, the woman and the man (3:14–19). But first, the scene begins with the LORD God walking in the garden in the cool of the day. He has not abandoned his creation, unlike in some African creation stories. But something has changed. Sin has spoiled the most precious thing of all – the relationship between humanity and God – and now the man and woman hide themselves from the *presence* of the LORD. We often only realize the closeness of our relationship to God when it is missing.

Having considered the matter carefully, the LORD God issues punishments or consequences to the serpent, the woman and the man which all strike at each one's identity (shrewdness, childbearing and work). The serpent will now become the most humble creature and the woman will experience pains in childbearing. The man will lose his profitable relationship to creation. The ground is cursed: it will not produce its crops except by painful hard work to the point of exhaustion. Thorns and thistles will grow in the maize, weeds that crowd out the crop and steal its nutrients. Finally, after all this painful toil, rather than enjoying the fruit of his labour, the man will die. The man was supposed to rule over the ground, but now the ground will swallow him up in death. The man and the woman were placed in the world to rule but now will be ruled. This is a story with which many African village farmers can identify. This describes subsistence farming, using all one's time and energy just to produce barely enough to feed the family. None of the abundance envisaged in Genesis 1–2!

Finally, the man and the woman are cast out of the garden and will now live in the desert, unable to fulfil their mission and calling.

Contribution to Community Development

Genesis 3 is hugely significant to understanding our efforts in community development. Through it, we learn why the world is in a mess and not as God created it. We learn why our progress is so difficult, why our crops fail and our animals die. We learn that humanity, not God, is to blame for the corruption of his good creation. The consequences of sin are immense, far-reaching and long-lasting. In fact, they result in community "*undevelopment*" as we see:

Sin undercuts community development. God made the first man, Adam, the representative for all humanity (Rom 5:15–19), so the impact of sin's entrance into the world is felt even by us today. Future generations will also have a sinful nature, enslaved to making poor choices, resulting in self-harm. Children inherit bad approaches and attitudes to life and work from their parents and the cycle of poverty continues. We are responsible for the breakdown of life in our community and the lack of harmony we experience cannot be put down to bad luck or angry ancestors.[17] At the same time, certain people's sin results in the exploitation of others.

Harmony and life are lost. The world is now characterized by separation. Harmony between God and humanity, harmony among people and harmony between humanity and the rest of creation are broken. Even our own self-understanding is broken with the image of God marred and distorted. And broken people break others and other things. There is now discord in marriage. Instead of husband and wife working in unison, they will now be unsupportive of one another, making producing a living on the cursed ground doubly hard. The root cause of our struggle to enjoy life is the broken relationships with God, self, others and the rest of creation, which intersect with one another. Consequently, we try to do things without God and his knowledge, which results for example in environmental destruction and the desert taking over

---

17. Chapter 4 will unpack this thought further.

the garden. What will be apparent is that *no technology will be able to break the curse of our poverty.*[18]

Authority is lost to the serpent. The man and woman handed over their authority to Satan. They were placed in the world to rule but will now be ruled. Humanity will now fail to live out its goal and purpose because of the effects of sin. Communities will be at the mercy of other things – poor climate, pests, unproductive soil and other people – as they try to eke out a living, having been *ejected* from the luscious garden.

There is hope amid despair. Although it appears otherwise, there is still hope! Among God's words of judgement to the woman are "And I will put enmity between you and the woman, and between your offspring and hers; he will crush your head, and you will strike his heel" (3:15). Here *God* himself places the hope of redemption *in the world* with the promise of the seed of the woman who will inflict the serpent's final defeat. And he provides a sacrifice to clothe the man and woman as they depart from the garden. Fortunately, this is not the end of the story. The mission given to humanity (Gen 1–2) need not be deleted but adjusted and expectations reset because of the fall.

The Spreading of Sin in the World Leads to Unhealthy Development: Genesis 4–11

As we read on from Genesis 3 it becomes apparent that redemption is not immediate. Instead, in chapters 4–11 we see the devastating effects of sin going viral throughout the whole world. We also see the beginning of the development of peoples and the beginning of human development and culture, but it is far from utopia, with the world becoming a violent place (still sadly common in some parts of Africa today). Cain misuses his field to murder his brother (4:8), tools are made for war (4:22), God floods the world because humanity has become so wicked (6:1 – 8:22), and even though he makes a covenant with all creation, restating his original blessing (9:1–17), humanity rebels against God's command to fill the earth and instead gathers in one place to build a tower to honour itself, only to be confused and broken up (11:1–9).

The Tower of Babel episode shows poignantly the failure of secular community development theories which believe that communities organizing

---

18. Western people may have tried to break this curse with technology but they have not succeeded in overcoming the full and deeper sense of poverty, which requires God's grace and our repentance!

themselves can achieve what they desire.[19] Rather, we see the value of communities organizing themselves under God's direction.

III. Calling of Abraham and Israel and Community Development

We have seen that human rebellion has caused the world to become a horrible place. God's judgement on the human race at Babel is drastic in breaking up humanity into separate peoples, scattering them across the face of the earth. This action seems to be intended to frustrate their plans and make life difficult for them. And so naturally we ask, is there now any hope for the world and its communities?

The Call of Abram: God's Response

God, the King of the earth, answers this question positively with his calling of Abram. He has not finished with his creation and the people he has made. In Genesis 12:1–3 he calls Abram in Ur of the Chaldeans, beginning, "Go from your country, your people and your father's household." Ur was a sophisticated and wealthy city with, as archaeology has uncovered, a well-developed urban culture.[20] But the city was also full of idolatry (Josh 24:2). God calls Abram to leave all this behind and go to the land he will show him. Just as God spoke creation into being (1:3), so he speaks again to create a new beginning, the creation of a new people (12:1). With the call of Abram, God begins the story of Israel as his covenant people. His original blessing on all humanity (1:28) is now given to Abram and his family.

But why is just this one family of the human race chosen and given the promise of blessing? The climax of God's words, "and all peoples on earth *will* be blessed through you" (12:3, emphasis added; cf. 3:15), reveals God's missional intent with this call as ultimately being of benefit for all nations – one people for all peoples! This is a fresh start for community development with this family called to live out being a people in the land of Canaan.

Abram is blessed to *be* a blessing. In Genesis, "blessing" means to be empowered to enjoy God and his goodness, and specifically empowered to fulfil the ordained roles to be fruitful and to rule (1:28). This means that Abram and his family are blessed to experience the healing of the four fundamental

19. So Gordon Wenham, *Rethinking Genesis 1–11: Gateway to the Bible*, Didsbury Lecture Series (Eugene: Cascade, 2015), 62.

20. D. A. Carson, ed., *NIV Zondervan Study Bible* (Grand Rapids: Zondervan, 2015), 45.

intersecting relationships – with God, with self, with others and with the rest of creation – which spreads to other peoples as they see the blessing in operation. It is a mission that now includes redemption.

Abram is promised *children* (to become a nation) and *land* (which includes space for crops and animals, and later for cities and businesses too). God's intent is for Abram and his descendants to move to this land and grow into a nation so as to *be* a model people. They are to bear his image and character and demonstrate the blessing that comes in following him so that the nations will see God and enter his blessing (cf. 18:18–19). In the agrarian culture of the day, transformed farming is essential to the modelling of life to the nations which God requires. As Abram and his family obey God, the abundant crops, fat cows and juicy fruit hanging on the trees will cause the nations to ask, "How is this possible?" The same can be true for us in Africa!

God's choice of Canaan is particularly interesting in terms of its climate and fertility. Humanly speaking, if one wanted to create the best demonstration farm, there were other places better suited. While there could be good rains, generally rainfall was erratic and there could be years of drought or abundance. God chooses a place where successful living will not be guaranteed but will be a result of the people's living in right relationship with him and the land.

Genesis 12 *begins* to answer a fundamental question of our human existence: what is the solution? It is that God has called Abram and his family to be his missional people, and as the family obey him and receive his blessing, thereby bearing his image and modelling the life he intended for humanity that others might see this life and wisdom and enter in, the effects of the fall begin to be reversed. In this way, we see God's people are to be agents of community transformation.

In the remainder of Genesis, although we tend to see the failings of this family, there are glimpses of the life God intended or of their being used to connect others with this life. In 13:1–18 we see that the LORD continues to bless Abram especially with livestock, so much so that he and his nephew Lot need to separate in order to find sufficient land for grazing their herds. Abram takes the initiative to resolve the conflict that had arisen between his and Lot's herdsmen, generously allowing Lot to choose his land first with Abram promising to go in the opposite direction. Lot looks and chooses what looks like "the garden of the LORD" (v. 10) in the area of Sodom and Gomorrah, the apparently better land. He follows Eve who also chose by sight, and like her he lives to regret his choice. In contrast, Abram settles in Canaan, the apparently poorer area. In response to Abram, the LORD then reiterates and expands his promise in terms of enlarged land and numerous offspring. What we learn is that poorer land with God is better than better land without him. After all, God can bless the poorer land and make it abundant.

Genesis 26 is a wonderful chapter which shows Isaac as Abraham's[21] true son, carrying on God's story beautifully as the rightful inheritor of the covenant promises. Although "there was a famine in the land" (v. 1), Isaac, following the LORD's instruction, stays and strikingly obtains an abundant crop, and enjoys God's blessings of wealth and many flocks, herds and servants (vv. 12–14). Isaac's huge blessing causes the nearby Philistines to envy him and leads into conflict over wells. Their aim is to hurt him and his flocks by closing wells during this time when water is scarce. What we then see is Isaac behaving wisely, avoiding quarrels, persevering through a cycle of moving away and reopening the wells, only for the wells to be contested again, until eventually he and his servants dig one which is not contested. Isaac names it "Rehoboth, saying, 'Now the LORD has given us room and *we will flourish in the land*'" (v. 22, emphasis added). The Philistines recognize God's continued blessing on Isaac and want peace. Isaac, though holding the upper hand in the discussions, does not abuse his power but makes peace with them (vv. 30–31) and in so doing allows the blessing of God to flow to them (cf. 12:3). These Philistines, men of Gerar, are allowed to find peace themselves when previously they had been the aggravators. The whole episode shows a mature Isaac in right relationship with God and seeking right relationships with others, living a life of faith and obedience in a challenging season, revealing God's blessing and wisdom to others, and being blessed accordingly by the LORD.

The end of the book of Genesis shows Joseph, Abraham's great-grandson, being used to avert widespread disaster in the communities of the then known world (Gen 41–50). As a humble, wrongly imprisoned Hebrew slave, he alone is wise enough to formulate an executive plan for Egypt to make provision during seven years of plenty in order that Egypt would not be ruined by the seven years of famine that followed. Amid this, he witnesses before Pharaoh to God's unique wisdom as he controls the future (41:16, 28–32). As Joseph executes the plan, the impact is amazing. "When the famine had spread over the whole country, Joseph opened all the storehouses and sold grain to the Egyptians, for the famine was severe throughout Egypt. And all the world came to Egypt to buy grain from Joseph, because the famine was severe everywhere" (41:56–57). Here we see Joseph fulfilling the call of God to his great-grandfather to be a blessing to the world and exercising stewardship over creation for the good

---

21. Abram's name is changed in Genesis 17 by God to "Abraham," meaning "father of many nations," picking up Genesis 12:3 and emphasizing the missional intent of his calling.

of the world through his careful supervision in the seven years of plenty. The story highlights the importance of the people of God being involved in high places in setting wise policies to benefit society and the poor in particular, both to aid good development and to make provision to avoid widespread disaster in times of drought. May the wise among God's people use their wisdom to bless their countries.

The Redemption of Israel from Egypt Serves God's Mission

The children of Israel joined Joseph in Egypt and were invited by Pharaoh to settle in the land of Goshen where they prospered. Later, the work of Joseph was forgotten and a new king, worried about the numerous Israelites, enslaved them to ruthless harsh labour. Christopher Wright describes their awful situation in terms of its political, economic, social and spiritual dimensions.[22] First, a new political situation arose under which they were treated differently from others with no voice to change things (Exod 1:8–10). Second, as slaves, they were exploited, having no property and no chance of running their own businesses (vv. 11–14). Third, there was pain and grief within the community as baby boys were murdered (vv. 15–22). And fourth, the Israelites' slavery prevented them fully serving and worshipping the LORD (4:22–23). As the story progresses from Egypt to the promised land, we see there is *full redemption* with God transforming all these dimensions, something we should be attentive to in our work among African communities.

God summons Moses and meets him at the burning bush to begin Israel's deliverance, saying to him,

> I have indeed seen the misery of my people in Egypt. I have heard them crying out because of their slave drivers, and I am concerned about their suffering. So I have come down to rescue them from the hand of the Egyptians and to bring them up out of that land into a good and spacious land, a land flowing with milk and honey – the home of the Canaanites, Hittites, Amorites, Perizzites, Hivites and Jebusites. And now the cry of the Israelites has reached me, and I have seen the way the Egyptians are oppressing them. So now, go. I am sending you to Pharaoh to bring my people the Israelites out of Egypt. (3:7–10)

---

22. Christopher Wright, *The Mission of God: Unlocking the Bible's Grand Narrative* (Downers Grove, IL: IVP Academic, 2006), 268–72.

The LORD is a God who "sees," "hears" and "is concerned" about his people (v. 7; cf. 2:24–25). He is an active God who "comes down" – not remaining far off as in many traditional African understandings of God – in order to deliver them from the Egyptians. In fact, God comes *down* to bring his people *up* into a new land, which is fertile and spacious. It is described as "overflowing with milk and honey," which symbolizes abundance and points to this land, originally given to Abraham, as a new garden of Eden, where Israel's life can be transformed.[23]

God's compassionate saving of Israel also serves his worldwide mission. Through this powerful deliverance his intent is that his name might be revealed to Israel (Exod 6:2–8) *and* proclaimed in all the earth (9:16, 29; cf. Josh 2:10–11). He thus begins the reconnection of his intimate relationship with humanity now through Israel, displaying his presence, character, mighty acts of power and glory to them, which will spiral out to the world.

God's Covenant with Israel for His Mission

After God redeems his people from Egypt, taking them through the Red Sea, he brings them to Mount Sinai and makes a covenant with them, inviting them, "Now then, if you will indeed obey My voice and keep My covenant, then you shall be My [treasured] possession among all the peoples, for all the earth is Mine; and you shall be to Me a kingdom of priests and a holy nation" (Exod 19:5–6 NASB). William Dumbrell explains this is a kind of commentary on Genesis 12:1–3; it tells us how Israel will fulfil God's promise of being a blessing to the nations.[24] The purpose of Israel's election is evident with "for all the earth is Mine." As a holy nation, Israel are to be like God. As a kingdom of priests, Israel are *both* to stand between God and the nations mediating his life to them and reflecting his holiness into the world, *and* to reign and display God's kingdom to others. *They are to be God's people who become a light and transforming presence to the nations.* In this way, the whole-life call to serve God's creation as rulers and priests is still in place.

God gives the law to frame Israel's response to his gracious deliverance. By following the law Israel can be his showcase people in the new garden of Eden. His instructions cover every area of life (e.g. family life, business ethics, worship, justice, care of animals, the land and property). We see two particular

---

23. The land is later described as Eden (Isa 51:3; Ezek 36:35; Joel 2:3).

24. William Dumbrell, *Covenant and Creation: A Theology of Old Testament Covenants* (Nashville: Thomas Nelson, 1984), 90.

emphases in the law which display the distinction of Israel's life to others: justice for the vulnerable and love for outsiders (e.g. Deut 10:12–22).[25] Taking up the cause of the powerless reveals the heart of God and is still a vital mark of any good community today. God desires his people to be a model people who bear his character – in wisdom, love, justice, compassion, mercy – so that the nations will see the advantages of his lived-out communal wisdom, do likewise and enter God's blessing (Deut 4:6). In this way, Israel serves God's mission of extending his kingdom in the world.

Israel Growing in the Land and Showing Signs of God's Blessing

As we continue into the next stage of Israel's story, we look for the type of community Israel becomes and how much they extend God's blessings to others.

Israel are settled well in the land under Joshua. Now with the law to guide them, they are supposed to live as a just and compassionate community so the nations will take notice. But the people become wayward after Joshua's death and in time Israel ask for a king so they will "be like all the other nations" (1 Sam 8:20). The only problem is they were supposed to be distinct, different from the other nations. How could they (and the African church today) live out their calling by being like everyone else! Once Samuel the prophet has set kingship within a covenantal framework (1 Sam 12:12–15; cf. Exod 19:5–6), we see David, a man after God's heart, in the main exercising godly leadership and facilitating God's kingship over and through Israel. He worships the LORD, displays compassion towards those with disabilities, does "what was just and right for all his people" (2 Sam 8:15), welcomes foreigners to his court and rules beyond the borders of Israel – all displaying Israel's community taking shape. He also brings the ark into Jerusalem, making it the city of God, to which the nations are later invited to learn of the LORD. When David wishes to build God a temple, God responds by promising David an everlasting dynasty with a son, like a new Adam, to rule the nations (2 Sam 7; cf. Ps 2; Dan 7:1–14). In this way, the vocation and hope of Israel become focused on David's son.

The peace and blessing established by David are extended by his son Solomon, who begins well by asking for wisdom and building the temple. For much of his reign Israel prosper under it, enjoying shalom as the phrase "everyone under their own vine and under their own fig-tree" evokes (1 Kgs 4:20–25). There is a partial fulfilment of being a blessing to the nations with

---

25. The motivation being remembering their own former slavery.

foreigners coming to hear his great wisdom (1 Kgs 4:34; cf. Deut 4:6). He even describes plant life and animals, birds, reptiles and fish (1 Kgs 4:29–34) – a gentle prod to the African church that God's wisdom is not to be thought of as confined to certain sectors.

Many of the Psalms and Proverbs come from this David-Solomon era. Proverbs shows the benefits of wisdom for thriving community relationships, achieved through respect for parents, wholesome marriages, hard work, honest business transactions and right treatment of the disadvantaged. The Psalms call the people of Israel to centre their lives on the LORD who alone makes their life viable. Even through the challenges of life, the people are urged to turn to him and offer him their allegiance and in so doing make his name known to all. He is the King of all the earth, who will one day come as Judge to make everything right in the world.

The Prophetic Perspective: Judgement and Hope for Renewal

Having spoken about God's vision and purpose for Israel and seen some glimpses of the vision being realized, we need to ask, how did it work out? How far did Israel fulfil their calling of being an exemplary community and participating in God's mission? And what can we learn for how the church should conduct itself so as to be a channel for transformation in Africa?

It comes as no surprise to learn that generally Israel failed to live up to their calling. We see this stemming even from the time of Joshua and the judges, though the book of Ruth is a welcome exception.[26] And the David-Solomon era is far from perfect. David's sons disappoint as kings and leaders, resulting in widespread failure among the people to follow God. The Old Testament prophets pick up this failing and deliver a stinging critique. They interpret the law in the present situation, explaining how Israel have violated the covenant and that the covenant curses will be enacted if they do not change. Let us look first at a few samples of their critique.

Amos and judgement because of injustice. Amos is a shepherd from Tekoa in Judah about 11 miles from Jerusalem and prophesies during the reigns of Uzziah of Judah and Jeroboam II of Israel (1:1). His oracles are addressed mostly to the northern kingdom, Israel, who are in a period of economic prosperity. However, alongside this prosperity has come idolatry, extravagant

---

26. The book of Daniel is a splendid later example of the people of God even in captivity being a light and blessing to the beast-like world. The book of Jonah however contains the story of a reluctant missionary!

living, selfish abuse of power and privilege, and hence injustice and oppression of the poor. Their idolatry and syncretistic religion have opened the door to unjust government and social disorder, which sells "the needy for a pair of sandals" and allows "father and son [to exploit] the same girl" (2:6–8). Amos's message is against the nation's complacency. It is time for them to "hear" the word of the LORD. He is like a roaring lion who will dry up the fertile land which had led to the prosperity (1:2). Although the prophet urges the people to repent and seek the LORD (5:1–17), they do not listen and so disaster will strike (3:11) and they will go into exile (6:7).

Isaiah and Jerusalem, the city of blood. Later Isaiah speaks poignantly to Judah of God's hiding his face when they spread out their hands in prayer because their hands are full of blood (1:10–15). They are urged to "learn to do right; seek justice. Defend the oppressed. Take up the cause of the fatherless; plead the case of the widow" (1:17). Jerusalem, the city of God, called to be a light to the nations (cf. 2:5), has become the city of blood, and so devastating judgement and exile will ensue (5:13).

The point of the prophets is that when God is not central, his vision does not guide the nation and they allow syncretistic religion to creep in, resulting in the breakdown of community life, God will not look the other way. This is no less true for us today!

But although judgement is severe, it is not the last word, and the restoration of God's people and their calling to follow will be even more spectacular!

Ezekiel and the new heart in the new garden of Eden. The prophet Ezekiel promises a special restoration in chapter 36. The people had previously used the mountains of Israel to place altars where they made sacrifices to foreign gods and idols (Ezek 6:1–4). God brought judgement upon them, ruining the land and making it unproductive. Sin had affected everything – community life, the harvests, the rainfall, their whole well-being! But chapter 36 reveals God's intention to restore his people and to heal everything which their sin has spoiled, not least the honour of his name. In verses 26–28, he promises to fix the problem once and for all as he resettles the people in the land, so they will not return to their old ways and dishonour him again.

> I will give you a new heart and put a new spirit in you; I will remove from you your heart of stone and give you a heart of flesh. And I will put my Spirit in you and move you to follow my decrees and be careful to keep my laws. Then you will live in the land I gave your ancestors; you will be my people, and I will be your God.

He will make them new people from the inside – new thinking, new attitudes, new motivation! A new orientation will lead to a new lifestyle, a God-filled lifestyle. He will give them a heart transplant and grant them his Spirit so they will obey him fully. The character of the community will be changed and a just social order established as the law imagined. God's transformation will even go beyond society, as he says,

> I will call for the corn and make it plentiful and will not bring famine upon you. I will increase the fruit of the trees and the crops of the field, so that you will no longer suffer disgrace among the nations because of famine . . . The desolate land will be cultivated instead of lying desolate in the sight of all who pass through it. They will say, "This land that was laid waste has become like *the garden of Eden*; the cities that were lying in ruins, desolate and destroyed, are now fortified and inhabited." (36:29b–30, 34–35, emphasis added)

God will use the restoration of his people and the land as the vehicle of his ultimate purpose that the nations around them might *know* that it is all God's doing (vv. 36–38).[27] As we allow God to do heart surgery in us today, giving us a new orientation to work with him in rebuilding and restoring life, he will be displayed as the true God for all to see.

Isaiah and the new creation. The broadest and most awe-inspiring vision of transformation comes in Isaiah's vision of the new heavens and a new earth (Isa 65:17–25; cf. 32:17–20; 35:1–10). This is not just the transformation of the land of Israel but the transformation of the whole cosmos to be a place of shalom. Sin has spoiled not just the promised land but the whole world. God begins, "See, I will create new heavens and a new earth. The former things will not be remembered, nor will they come to mind" (65:17). God promises to create a new permanent joyful order where there is no memory of the old painful one (vv. 18–19). What is clear is that salvation is not merely renovation; it is transformation! The city will be a place of health, long life, building and fruitful work where the curse of Genesis 3 is removed and Eden restored (vv. 20–23).

Most of all, they will enjoy intimate fellowship with God (v. 24) and there will be no threat at all in and to Zion (v. 25). Isaiah's inaugural vision of 2:1–5 is remembered when Israel will no longer have to go out to war in defence of their land but will be able to turn "swords into ploughshares" (Isa 2:4; cf. Joel 3:10;

---

27. For the eschatological ingathering of the nations, see e.g. Isa 2:2–5; 45:22–23; 49:6; 56:6–7; Zech 8:20–23; 9:10.

Mic 4:3). It will then be a time when God's people, believing Jews and Gentiles alike (cf. Isa 49:1–6; 56:1–8), will enjoy unhindered and productive cultivation of crops and fruit in well-watered gardens and pasture for their animals (cf. Isa 30:23; Joel 2:23–27). But the prophet has already said this will come through the work of an Anointed One who will be a son of David (Isa 61; cf. 9:6–7; 11:1–9; 55:3; Jer 23:5–6). We look at him and his work in the next chapter.

In summary, the prophets envisage a huge and thorough renewal, particularly through the coming of the Messiah and a new temple. Indeed, this new temple is connected to the restoration of creation, where the water of life flows from the temple into the parched land (Ezek 47; cf. Gen 2:10–14). The prophets see God's restoration of the world as transforming the brokenness between us and God into rich relationship, transforming human society (community in the land) and transforming the rest of creation.

Contribution to Community Development

The long, wandering story of Israel has much to teach the people of God today about community development, and though many themes and principles have already been noted in our journey, I draw out a few key insights now.

The people of God have a missional identity, demonstrating an integrated and in situ witness. Mission is not a thing God's people do, or even a department of the church; it is about *who we are.* It is in our DNA. The story of Israel reveals that witness is an integrated witness covering the whole of life. Whatever we are doing or saying and wherever it is taking place, the world is watching and gaining a true or false picture of God and his intentions. Furthermore, the witness has a context, in the Old Testament being worked out in the land of Israel. The African church should consider its contexts and locations where it is gathered and scattered, with their opportunities and needs, and use these for concrete expressions of integrated witness. The church should allow its passion for community development to arise from its missional identity and to flow from and be connected with its overall mission to partner with God to see his kingdom come.

The world needs the multidimensional wisdom of the people of God. Although we can sometimes be dismissive of what the church has to offer, the world desperately needs wisdom for life. Moses reminded Israel that if they followed the LORD's commands, the effect would take root in their life and the nations would see their inherent wisdom (Deut 4:6). The desire of the nations to learn the wisdom of the people of God comes to fruition in the life of King Solomon, who *was given wisdom* by God (1 Kgs 4:29). He taught key insights on a variety of topics to the foreign delegates who came because of the shalom his kingdom was enjoying. By living in the fear of the LORD and being eager to learn and receive wisdom in family life, finances, gender empowerment, education and so on, the church in Africa will have gained valuable, and sought after, wisdom to share. We should be careful to learn from Solomon whose eventual downfall was due to separating wisdom from the fear of the LORD (cf. Prov 9:10). Instead, let us remain humble before God, even as we set our minds on learning knowledge and wisdom.

The people of God should be concerned with integrity, justice, the disadvantaged and the outsider. As a model people, the people of God are to be concerned with their integrity with God and in their relationships with one another and ensure that there is justice for all, not taking advantage of the vulnerable. As we saw, the lack of integrity and justice was Israel's downfall. Injustice in God's people is an affront to the God of justice. The church must therefore be honest where it is, being a model also of how it deals with injustice, both in the wider community and with its own shortcomings. There can be no real community development if corruption in the church and the love of money and material things are not brought into the light and dealt with. But when the church involves itself as a *life-giving community* in its villages, towns and cities, the results can be dramatic.

We have a close relationship with the land. We see that the life of God's people is intricately connected to their land. Development often comes from a flourishing land and in contrast the land suffers because of the people's sins. Indeed, if communities are to enjoy wholeness and well-being (shalom), then it will be a holistic shalom. May the church reflect on this, repenting of its sins, so that its land and resources can be well utilized to facilitate flourishing communities. And at a time when, because of the current ecological crisis, many are asking the question raised at the end of the journey through Genesis 1–11, "Is there now any hope for the world and its communities?," the church has an opportunity to be a "new Abraham."

As we will see, the New Testament does not forget these points but builds upon and extends them to lead to more glorious communities.

3

Community Development within the Overarching Story of God's Mission (Part 2)

The Story Continued, Not Abandoned!

We sometimes fail to appreciate that the New Testament picks up where the Old Testament finishes, even though in our canonical books there is a gap of four hundred years between the Testaments. As we enter the New Testament section of God's story of mission, we will see how it picks up so many of the threads, both the ideas and the hopes, and reworks them and shows their fulfilment. We begin with Jesus, the long-awaited and long-hoped-for Messiah, who breathes fresh life into the vision for thriving communities enjoying God and his goodness.

IV. Christ, the Kingdom and Community
Introduction to Jesus

Israel, at the time of Jesus, are in a complete mess. The people are suffering under the harsh foreign rule of the Romans, their own leaders are compromised and corrupt, Israel as a whole have not returned home and to the Lord, and God's presence has not come to the rebuilt temple. The glorious return, the new exodus, and the restoration envisaged by the prophets are therefore yet to happen.[1] The people, called to bring God's salvation to the world, need a Saviour themselves.

---

1. Even the picture we see in Ezra and Nehemiah and the post-exilic prophets of Haggai, Zechariah and Malachi is not of the glorious return imagined.

As we will see, the coming of Jesus into the world is what turns the whole biblical story from disaster to triumph. When things become impossible, the King comes himself. Because of Jesus, the story of the Bible, which began with creation but tragically ran into trouble along the way, can now reach God's intended goal of his temple-kingdom filling the entire world (cf. Hab 2:14). As we examine Jesus's life and impact, there are two interrelated questions we need to consider: Who is he? And what is his mission? We turn to consider these now.

Jesus's Identity Is Seen in His Beginnings (Matthew 1; Mark 1; Luke 1–2)

As the New Testament opens, anticipation is raised with its very first line: "This is the genealogy of Jesus the Messiah the son of David, the son of Abraham" (Matt 1:1). Here is Jesus, as true son of Abraham and true son of David, who will enable the blessing of Abraham to flow to the nations and will be the Son of God, reigning for ever on David's throne in fulfilment of the Scriptures (Matt 1; Luke 1; cf. 2 Sam 7). It is clear: the earlier chapters of the biblical story have not been forgotten or discarded but are about to be fulfilled.

As Mark records the beginning of Jesus's ministry, he links it to Israel's deliverance by drawing on Isaiah 40:3 which evoked Israel's redemption from Egypt and journey through the wilderness, showing that a similar but greater exodus is about to occur in Jesus (Mark 1:2–11). A voice from heaven declares, "You are my Son, whom I love; with you I am well pleased" (Mark 1:11). This powerful statement, wrapping up several Old Testament scriptures, reveals who Jesus is – God's unique son (Gen 22), true Israel (Exod 4:22) and Messiah (Isa 11; 42) – who is taking up Israel's story and vocation into himself as messianic true servant Israel. And as Son, he truly bears God's image (cf. Col 1:15; Heb 1:2). The image, lost at the fall, makes a spectacular reappearance in the life and ministry of Jesus, the Son of Man.[2]

Jesus's Ministry and Mission Are All about the Kingdom of God

As Jesus begins his ministry, he announces in Mark 1:14–15, "The time has come. . . . The kingdom of God has come near. Repent and believe the good

---

2. "Son of Man" is Jesus's favourite self-identifying term and is likely drawn from Dan 7:13–14, where "one like a son of man" is given authority to inflict total defeat on evil, will then be vindicated and will receive an everlasting kingdom. For our purposes, it particularly emphasizes Jesus's humanity as the truly human one, who is also the new Adam and shows his solidarity with people, including suffering as the means of fulfilling Daniel 7.

news!" This is the gospel, the good news, which Matthew expands as "the good news of the kingdom" (Matt 4:23), lest we miss the point. Jesus here in Mark 1 is in effect saying to his hearers, "What you have all been waiting for, the reign of God, I am bringing here right now. So line up your lives with me and the kingdom now!" Here he is as messianic king through whom God is present and will reign, dealing with evil and healing the brokenness of his people, the nations and creation so that his just and peaceable kingdom will eventually fill the earth (cf. 2 Sam 7; 1 Chr 28–29; Pss 2; 72; Isa 9:6–7; 11:1–9).

Indeed, Jesus's ministry and mission are all about the kingdom of God and it is through this lens of the kingdom that his person, life and purpose come into focus. God is ruling through him and his work touches everything. What Adam and Eve lost through the fall – the ability to rule over creation and bring God's blessing to it – Jesus regains and makes available to those who believe in him. We see Jesus embodying God's reign and proclaiming it powerfully in word and deed. We see him ruling over creation, the demonic, death and sickness (e.g. Mark 4:35 – 5:43). All of these are signs that God's order is being put back into this world through Jesus.

Jesus, anointed by the Spirit, launches his radical kingdom agenda in Nazareth, promising good news to the poor and oppressed, to liberate[3] them through a new exodus and to set a new just order in place, even beyond the borders of Israel (Luke 4:14–30; cf. Isa 61:1–2). Simeon had foretold that Jesus would be "a light for revelation to the Gentiles" (Luke 2:32; cf. Isa 42:6; 49:6). Jesus offers a profound insight into the nature of God through his enaction of the Year of Jubilee, with the poor, enslaved and oppressed now centre stage (cf. Lev 25). This agenda he continues unperturbed through increasing opposition (Luke 11:14–54).

The Kingdom Is Ultimately Established in Jesus's Death

Having proclaimed the kingdom around Galilee, Jesus resolutely sets out for Jerusalem in order to complete his mission (Luke 9:51). Jerusalem, the city of God but at that time corrupted, is where the decisive battle takes place between the kingdom of God and the powers of darkness. Here we see the realization of Daniel's vision where "one like a son of man" defeats the beastly powers and is granted an everlasting kingdom (Dan 7). Jesus has already challenged Israel's way of being, not least in their "beastly" exploitation of the poor and

---

3. The idea of liberator figures is common in African cultures (see Healey and Sybertz, *African Narrative Theology*, 64–69).

lack of concern to be a light to the Gentiles. And the opposition continues to mount to the point of his crucifixion. But Jesus achieves his victory as the Suffering Servant in his sacrificial death for the world (Luke 22:1 – 23:56; cf. Isa 52:13 – 53:12).[4] This is the way evil is defeated – not by fighting evil with evil. He fulfils his stated goal: "For even the Son of Man did not come to be served, but to serve, and to give his life as a ransom for many" (Mark 10:45). This is the most God-like act! On the cross, he is enthroned as king and cries, "It is finished" (John 19:30). The cross is thus God's amazing cosmic victory. The "beasts" are overthrown and the kingdom established (cf. Dan 7:13–14). God's order is reinstituted, as Jesus, the Son of Man, crushes the head of the serpent (cf. Gen 3:15).

Having outlined Jesus's life and mission, let us now delve deeper into his mission to draw out the aspects especially pertinent to our purposes.

Jesus's Mission as Integral Mission

If the African church is to be serious about integral mission, then it should *contemplate Jesus* as the practitioner par excellence! As we study Jesus's kingdom ministry to people, we see God's powerful presence and rule as he transforms whole lives. He beautifully and seamlessly integrates the meeting of their physical, spiritual and social needs as *whole* needs. When a paralysed man is brought to him, Jesus shockingly begins by saying, "Son, your sins are forgiven" (Mark 2:5), doing what only God can do as he reconnects the man to God, even calling him "son" and drawing him into God's family. But with the religious leaders aghast, he demonstrates his authority to forgive sins by healing the man physically, leaving everyone stunned and exclaiming, "We have never seen anything like this!" (Mark 2:12).

One day, Jesus meets a man born blind, and after assuring his disciples that this blindness is not the result of the man's or his parents' sin, he opens his eyes as the "light of the world" (John 9:1–5). But when the man is picked up and questioned by the Pharisees, it is clear he does not know who Jesus is (vv. 11–12). However, as the interrogation continues, he begins to see something of who Jesus is, calling him "a prophet" (vv. 17, 30–33). His eyes are "opening

---

4. Jesus's self-giving for the whole world transcends African notions of sacrifice and mediation (see Diane B. Stinton, *Jesus of Africa: Voices of Contemporary African Christology* [Maryknoll: Orbis, 2004], 109–42).

wider."[5] Later, Jesus hears that the man has been thrown out of the synagogue, and in his concern for this outcast searches after him (vv. 34–38). On finding him, Jesus says, "Do you believe in the Son of Man?" When the man asks, "Who is he?," Jesus replies, "You have now *seen* him [after all, Jesus opened his eyes]; in fact, he is the one speaking with you" (v. 37). The man says simply, "Lord, I believe," and he worships him (v. 38). Jesus is truly the light of the world as the man now fully sees. Jesus does not force things but goes at a natural pace. Similarly, when he feeds the five thousand with physical bread, satisfying their physical hunger, the next day he declares to them, "I am the bread of life" (John 6:35), offering to satisfy their spiritual hunger.

When Jesus is on his way to Jerusalem, close to the border between Samaria and Galilee, ten men with leprosy meet him as he is about to enter a village. Standing at a distance, they call out, "Jesus, Master, have pity on us!" (Luke 17:11). Surprisingly, he simply replies, "Go, show yourselves to the priests," and on their way to doing so they discover that their skin is cleansed. Moses had laid out strict rules, administered by the priests, for those with infectious diseases to socially distance, and specifying how they were to re-enter the community if they should be healed (Lev 13:9–17; 14:1–20; cf. Luke 5:14). So Jesus, by telling them to comply with these regulations, ensures they are healed not only physically but also in terms of their standing within the community. One of them, a despised Samaritan, returns to Jesus, this time falling at his feet, to thank him. Jesus turns to address those around him and points to God's astonishing work in this foreigner, so that the miracle impacts them too. Finally, he says to the man, "Rise and go; your faith has made you [whole/saved you[6]]" (v. 19). Now the man's healing is complete – physically, socially and spiritually.

Meeting Jesus produced dramatic effects on people. When Jesus singles out the deplorable rich chief tax collector Zacchaeus, and invites himself to receive Zacchaeus's hospitality, showing God's undeserved acceptance of him, what results? Zacchaeus responds with a whole-life reorientation by putting his corrupt life right. This is what salvation looks like: a transformed life (Luke 19:1–10).

---

5. George R. Beasley-Murray, *John*, Word Biblical Commentary 36 (Nashville: Thomas Nelson, 1987), 157.

6. The Greek word used here is *sōzō*, the usual word used for "to save," and is clearly intended to mean more than "to make well" as most English translations have, including the NIV.

Jesus: Incarnational Mission and Community

John 1:1–18 sets Jesus's coming as the beginning of a new creation, with the climax being, "The Word became flesh and made his dwelling among us. We have seen his glory, the glory of the one and only Son, who came from the Father, full of grace and truth" (1:14). The eternal God becomes a human being. To achieve his mission, God sends, not a message or a video, but a messenger – an embodied Word, full of grace and truth. In Jesus, God enters our world and reveals God's glory. God reveals his glory to us in the best possible way for us to comprehend – as a person seen in the flesh! In front of people in a way that they could see with their own eyes and touch with their own hands, Jesus demonstrates what God is like (cf. 1:18). Jesus journeys with people; he sits with them, he eats with them, he stays with them, just as God's tabernacle had gone with the Israelites through the desert to the promised land.

Throughout the gospels we see Jesus bringing the good news to the "wrong" people – Gentiles, women, prostitutes, sinners and tax collectors, the poor, the outcast and the marginalized. As they encounter him, they are changed and many stay with him as they follow and serve him as part of his travelling community. Even Jesus's choice of his twelve disciples, who are to serve as representatives of a new community to carry forth the mission of God, is surprising and ground-breaking. The new community inaugurated in Jesus is a socially diverse and ethnically boundary-breaking community, marked by allegiance to him, equal status, self-denial, love for one another and openness to the outsider. In terms of community development, Jesus redraws our imagination. And all of this is for the purpose of this community participating in his mission.

Returning to John 1, we see the deliberate echoes of the creation story – "in the beginning," creation through word, light and life, and climactically in the offer to become "children of God" (v. 12), akin to the image of God.[7] As the gospel proceeds, we see the fall is being undone: our relationship with God, with self, with others and with the rest of creation is being restored. And Jesus commissions his disciples, "As the Father has sent me, so I am sending you" (John 20:21; cf. 17:18). We are being called to do mission *in the same way* – humbly, vulnerably, fully – by entering people's worlds as an embodied Word-community, as we participate in the life of the Godhead. Jesus gives his disciples, and us too, his authority to carry on his new creation mission to form and to fill his world, through making disciples who are formed to be like

---

7. Children in the ancient world were to resemble or image their parents in character and actions (cf. Matt 5:43–48).

him and filled with his life (Matt 28:18–20; Luke 24:45–49; John 20:21–23). We are called to follow the Suffering Servant Messiah into the world, bearing his image, revealing his glory, and in the power of his Spirit implement the victory of his kingdom.

Contribution to Community Development

Jesus's life and mission led to the formation of a new community for the mission of God. His contribution to community development is thus immense, and I draw out the following reflections, though so many more could be given.

Community development has no chance without Jesus! Jesus is the centrepiece of God's whole story and the one who dealt with the evil holding back people and communities. There is no chance of significant community development if he is not at the centre of the community and its initiatives. His life was marked by self-giving, humility, dependence on God in prayer, the Spirit, love, truth, the right use of power and showing the true image of God. And he desires his people to have the same marks and bear this same image, his image, as a community with and for the world. He gives the church the resources for doing his work in his life and death. And yet, sadly, the church sometimes forgets Jesus in its efforts to work with communities, such as installing water supply systems without revealing the source of the water of life. May the church not be captive to the agendas of donors since there is no transformational mission and development apart from him!

Jesus connected sincerely with ordinary people. Jesus's life was intimately connected with people, particularly the needy and desperate. He invested significant time in people. He dignified people. He identified with people. He showed great compassion but at the same time was not scared to confront. He challenged the power structures that held the community back, being interested only in doing God's will and in his agenda, not allowing himself to be bought by political agendas as is sometimes the case in Africa. The church will do well in community development when it is a people *among* the community and *for* the community.

Jesus lived the message. As the Word made flesh, Jesus lived the message of God and his all-embracing kingdom. At no point do we see a disconnect between the way he lived and what he said and did. His words explained his actions and his actions demonstrated the sincerity of his words. He went to extremes, breaking social and political taboos, and was willing even to suffer to implement his mission. What cultural taboos does the church in Africa need to break in order to live the message? As the church truly embraces Jesus wherever it is, the message of his concern for people and communities will ooze out of the church and it will become the good news.

Jesus has renewed our creation mandate. Jesus, the Son of Man, through his work on the cross, has given us his authority to continue his work. Being his community is set within God's larger creational purposes, whereby we are sent out in the power of the Spirit on a truly integral and kingdom mission to see communities and creation experience God's new day.

V. Church: The Community of the King and the Kingdom

The gospels end and the book of Acts begins with the Risen Jesus. The resurrection is the most momentous event which takes everyone by surprise. Its impact will in time reverberate in every place.[8] The world will never be the same again. Jesus's resurrection is God's vindication of him. After all, would God have resurrected a false or failed messiah? This means that the cross is the ultimate victory and *the kingdom of God has indeed been established!* Furthermore, *the story of Israel has been fulfilled in the story of Jesus!* As Israel's true Messiah, Jesus is also the world's true King! This is the gospel which calls for allegiance to Jesus from all people. As they commit themselves to him, they become part of his people, the church, and begin to enjoy his benevolent reign while holding it out to others. How this story continues is the topic of Acts and the rest of the New Testament, culminating in Jesus's return to earth (cf. Acts 1:11) and the consummation of the kingdom of God. As we journey through the next stage of the story, let us see how God's vision for thriving and expanding communities comes into being, and be alert for how it can take root through us the church in Africa's villages, towns and cities today.

Acts: A Community Witnessing to Jesus Christ as Lord

The early chapters of Acts describe the birth of the church where the Spirit forms the church as a witnessing community to Jesus. The writer, Luke, begins by explaining that his first book (his gospel) was about "all that Jesus *began* to do and to teach until the day he was taken up to heaven" (Acts 1:1–2, emphasis added). Hence, by implication, Acts is about "all that Jesus *continues* to do and teach" from heaven, *by* the Holy Spirit, *through* the church. In this way, the church's mission is a continuation of Jesus's own mission and the shape,

---

8. Some African tribes, such as the Maasai, do not believe in an afterlife, so the resurrection cuts to the core of their identity (see Healey and Sybertz, *African Narrative Theology*, 77).

manner, substance and priorities of his earthly mission are to be the shape, manner, substance and priorities of our mission too. Jesus calls his disciples, as representatives of the church, to *be* his witnesses (Acts 1:8), not simply to *do* witnessing! The church's witness is therefore an identity issue.

In Acts 2, the Ascended Jesus, now on the throne of heaven, pours out the Holy Spirit, fulfilling Old Testament prophecy (Joel 2:28–32; Ezek 36:26–27; cf. Luke 3:16), which means, as the resurrection also displays, that the "last days" are now here. *Believers, as resurrected people, are filled with God's own presence* (cf. Ezek 37; Gen 2:7), *and therefore are now empowered to be God's missional people in the world* (Acts 2:5–11). We see the Spirit forming a missional community, with devoted discipleship, worship, prayer, signs and wonders, mutual care and care for the poor being marks of this community (2:42–47). For instance, a marginalized person with disabilities is dramatically healed in Jesus's name (3:1–10), the believers are "one in heart," sharing their possessions with "no needy person among them" (4:32–37), and the church ensures justice and mercy for the Hellenistic widows (6:1–4). We see those who have experienced the forgiveness of sins and the gift of the Spirit become a new inclusive community which exhibits the character of God. The consequence is "And *the Lord added* to their number daily those who were being saved" (2:47, emphasis added).

The church thus becomes an authentic and authenticating community for the gospel. On the Day of Pentecost, Peter had said, "God has made this Jesus, whom you crucified, both Lord and Messiah" (2:36). The early chapters demonstrate this community displaying in their lives that Jesus Christ is Lord come what may. It is a powerful and provocative witness, which goes hand in hand with the work of the apostles and leaders. Leadership in the church is marked by boldness, openly refusing to submit to Jewish authorities (4:19–20), with consistent *bold* and *storied* preaching (3:12 – 4:12, 33; 5:19–20; 13:16–41; 17:22–34). The gospel is seen to be powerful in word and deed, with preaching and healing together (8:4–7), and which confronts the powers, showing the superiority of God's power (8:7; 16:16–18).

The Acts story is one of movement and expansion, with Luke frequently inserting summaries of the continued spread of the Word (6:7; 9:31; 12:24; 16:5; 19:20). By the end of the book, we can see that the programme set out in 1:8[9] has been significantly but not fully executed, with the gospel being taken from the city of God (Jerusalem) to the city of the world (Rome).

---

9. This is very similar to the Great Commission (Matt 28:18–20).

Mission and a Church-Planting Movement

We see in Acts *church planting* being the early church's response, as they are empowered by the Holy Spirit, to Jesus's commissioning of them (Matt 28:18–20; Luke 24:45–49; John 20:21–23). Being obedient to his commission involves (1) evangelizing in new places and among new peoples and baptizing them both in water and in the Holy Spirit, and (2) gathering the new converts into new communities for discipling and teaching, worship, prayer, breaking of bread and bearing witness in word and life.

A church-planting movement emerges with believing communities being established wherever the apostles, leaders and church members go (in Jerusalem and Judea, among Samaritans under persecution, with God-fearing Gentiles and finally with Gentiles in Asia and Europe). Adaptation[10] takes place as the gospel crosses boundaries since the aim is a vibrant, genuine, relevant and local community of witness, just as Jerusalem was intended to be in the Old Testament. Antioch is a shining example of such a radical and mixed community, rooted in the word and prayer, impacting their city in holistic witness and sending forth missionaries to new places (Acts 11–13). So, Acts reveals the church as a community of witness, among which and from which the gospel radiates in life, word and deed.

Epistles: The Church as a Living Expression of the Gospel

While many Pentecostal churches in Africa draw much inspiration for mission from the book of Acts, and rightly so, the same sadly cannot be said of them when it comes to the New Testament Epistles. I hope in this section and the next to show that these Epistles are equally important for mission and, appreciated in unity with Acts, can lead to a *three-dimensional mission* among communities that desperately need good news.

When we come to the Epistles, we should see them as being written within the Acts framework of missional expansion. Paul and Peter, for example, write to their churches as missionaries on the road or in prison. Michael Gorman, in his wonderful book *Becoming the Gospel: Paul, Participation and Mission*,[11] has shown how to read Paul and the Pauline letters missionally. Once we read these Epistles within this missional framework, we see that, though written

---

10. E.g. the Acts 15 Council's decision promotes the unity of the church without compromise and with continued spread of the gospel.

11. Michael Gorman, *Becoming the Gospel: Paul, Participation and Mission* (Grand Rapids: Eerdmans, 2015).

with various issues and situations in mind, they ultimately serve to facilitate the churches to be gospel partners (cf. Phil 1:5), to be a living expression of the gospel and to spread its influence. That is why Paul is desperate to see his *passion for the poor* worked out in the churches' collection for the saints to show *one Lord, one gospel* and *one church* (1 Cor 16:1–4; 2 Cor 8–9; Rom 15:25–31). And it is why James too is keen to see social justice as a feature of the church. I will examine just a few epistles to see what they communicate about the mission of the church and how the church conducts this mission.

In the book of Ephesians, the writer inspires the church to be a people caught up in God's cosmic mission. To the church, God has unveiled his worldwide plan to bring all things together in Christ (1:10). This is a new arrangement for the uniting of the whole cosmos in Christ, whereby everything is brought together to work properly under the lordship of Jesus Christ, who is over all powers (1:22; 4:15; 5:23; cf. Col 1:19–20). God's intent in revealing this plan is for the church to participate in it as a reconciled and united people, God's stunning corporate masterpiece (2:10),[12] which discloses his multicoloured wisdom to the powers and rulers (3:10).[13] The church's role in this mission is progressed through three metaphors: the church as *the body of Christ*, as *the new humanity* and as *the temple of the Spirit*. First, as the body of Christ, we are the fullness of Christ who fills the world completely through us, the church (1:23). This highlights the importance of the church's relationship to its head, Jesus. It receives direction and nourishment from its head to engage in the mission of filling the world by growing together into his likeness and fullness and bearing his image in the world (4:11–13). Second, as the new humanity (2:15), bearing God's likeness "in true righteousness and holiness" (4:24), we are no longer defined by old identities – Jew or Gentile, black or white, Hutu or Tutsi, rich or poor, educated or uneducated, young or old, male or female, able-bodied or with disabilities. Now we are one new people in Christ our peace, reconciled in him, walking in good works. In this way, we are a preview of what God will do for all creation. Third, as the temple of the Spirit, we are being built together, to be full of God's presence (2:21–22; cf. 5:18), the joining

12. For a fuller treatment of this applied to a particular African situation, see Timothy J. Monger and Marco Methuselah, "God's Masterpiece: Ephesians 2:11–22 as Inspiration for the Church's Involvement in Peacemaking and Reconciliation with People with Albinism in Tanzania," in *Forgiveness, Peacemaking and Reconciliation*, Africa Society of Evangelical Theology Series 5, eds. Rodney L. Reed and David K. Ngaruiya (Carlisle: Langham Global Library, 2020), 103–26.

13. As Ernest Best says, "the reconciliation of Jews and Gentiles in the church is a kind of pilot scheme for a much greater reconciliation in which the powers will in turn be embraced." (*Ephesians*, International Critical Commentary [Edinburgh: T&T Clark, 1998], 326).

of heaven and earth, so that life flows to the barren places outside and the temple continues to grow. In this way, the church embodies and participates in God's world-remaking mission (4:10; 5:8–17; 5:21 – 6:9; 6:15–20).

Paul writes to the church in Philippi, a Roman colony, to further their "partnership in the gospel." As a Roman colony, Philippi was an outpost of Rome, exemplifying the life of Rome and spreading its influence in the province of Macedonia. Paul however sees the church as a colony of heaven (1:27; 3:20). He, a Roman citizen but self-identifying as a "slave of Christ Jesus" (1:1), urges the church to "live out your citizenship in a manner worthy of the gospel of Christ" (1:27), which is to stand firm as one in the face of opposition and suffering (1:28–30) by living the story of Christ's mission (2:5–11) and in so doing shining as stars into a dark world (2:16).[14] I believe this is an untapped invitation to African churches that by living out Christ's service and humiliation their light will shine brighter.

Both these letters, to the Ephesians and the Philippians, emphasize that the life of the church is intrinsically missional as the church is an embodied expression of the gospel for the world to see (cf. John 1:14). The letters also remind us that the creation story is reenergized and to be carried forward by the new humanity, the people of the second Adam, as they participate in him and his creation-wide kingdom programme.

Epistles: The Church Spreading the Goodness of Jesus's Kingship

We have seen from Ephesians and Philippians that the church is to be a living demonstration of the gospel which draws the world to its Saviour Jesus. But the church's mission is to be "a seamless witness of word and life."[15] When the gospel is authentically lived out by the church, questions will be asked, and the church is expected to tell outsiders the story behind its life and actions (1 Thess 1:7–8; Eph 6:15; Col 4:5–6). It is as a combination of word and life that the church is most effective in its witness.

The church is to be not just attractive in its witness but active in spreading the goodness of Jesus's kingship. We see this clearly in the letter of 1 Peter.[16] Peter writes to displaced people, "foreigners and exiles" (1:1, 17; 2:11) –

---

14. Translations in this sentence are my own, although strictly speaking in 1:1 Paul refers to himself and Timothy as "slaves of Christ."

15. Dean Flemming, *Recovering the Full Mission of God: A Biblical Perspective on Being, Doing and Telling* (Downers Grove: InterVarsity Press 2013), Kindle loc. 3478.

16. 1 Thessalonians, through its emphasis on the church's embodying faith, love and hope, has a similar approach.

an experience of many in Africa today. But he probably loads these terms theologically to distance them ideologically from their surrounding culture and to have their identity shaped by their being chosen by God to be his distinct people in the world. These readers, having come to Jesus, are being built into a Spiritual[17] house – a living temple (2:4–8). They have a unique status – a chosen people, a royal priesthood, a holy nation, a people for God's possession[18] – and are charged with Israel's calling "that you may declare the praises [or virtues] of him who called you out of darkness into his wonderful light" (2:9–10). This "declaring" (expanded in 2:11 – 4:19) is probably in life, word and deed. Peter next shows how their identity functions as the church lives among and is connected to a watching world (i.e. the living temple serves like Eden); namely, "to abstain from sinful desires, which wage war against your soul. Live such good lives among the pagans that, though they accuse you of doing wrong, they may see your good deeds and glorify God on the day he visits us" (2:11–12).

The goal of their good conduct, arising from their identity, is the conversion of outsiders (cf. Matt 5:16). They are to do good deeds to the outsiders in their contexts (1 Pet 2:15, 18, 20; 3:1, 9, 13, 17), as they follow in Jesus's steps and sometimes suffer the consequences. Of such a community, radically transformed by the gospel to be utterly different, shaped by their living hope and continually doing good to their society, questions will be asked. And so they must be always ready "to give [gently and respectfully] an answer to everyone who asks you to give the reason for the hope that you have" (3:15), with a confidence they will win some.

Whether or not the church is working among some of Africa's displaced peoples, 1 Peter highlights that God's people fulfil their calling by not being "at home" with the culture *and* by being well connected to it.

Contribution to Community Development

In addition to our survey of the church above, there are several important contributions to community development worth explicitly underlining here.

The church must work at integrating its life, service and mission into a whole. The church has a centripetal role (having an attractive life displaying the life of God) and a centrifugal role (evangelism, church planting and service in

---

17. I have capitalized "Spiritual" to show that they are being built into a house of the Spirit himself, as is surely the author's intention, rather than some general "spiritual house."

18. All these are descriptors of Israel (see Exod 19:6; Deut 7:6; 10:15; 1 Sam 12:22; Isa 62:12).

the community) which when operating in tandem enable the church to be an effective missional community.[19] The being, doing and telling of mission need to be in unison, reinforcing one another. In this way, the church will be a hermeneutic of the gospel, translating the gospel as a lived expression in a variety of ways and settings, and providing a full narrative of transformation to its community.

The church is to be a counter-cultural extended family. The church is a family of different peoples and tribes and takes the place of the traditional African extended family in the lives of its members. The focus in the New Testament is on the corporate nature of the church, being one body, offering the world an alternative community through humility, self-giving, love and opportunity for all, concern for the weak, justice modelled, transformed relationships and being welcoming to others. The church should realize that community development happens through being a transformed community!

The church is offered a magnificent role in society. The New Testament offers a big role for the church in society or among communities, particularly in reflecting Christ by doing good and working towards remaking the world as a place of peace and justice according to God's design in Christ. We would do well to reflect deeply on passages such as Ephesians 1:9–10; Colossians 1:15–23; Romans 8:18–27; and 1 Peter 2:11 – 3:17, and then, following the Spirit's leading, to improvise with a contextualized implementation, recognizing that such work will never be complete before Jesus returns.

VI. Consummation: The King Returns, the Kingdom Finalized and All Things Made New

The Bible looks forward to the consummation of the kingdom (e.g. Rom 8; 1 Pet 1; 2 Pet 3). And the church is a sign, instrument and foretaste of this kingdom. At times the church succeeds in this role. But at others, as the Epistles show, the calling is not carried out very well, often because of trouble and strife within the church community, sometimes because of acquiescing to the prevailing culture. The book of Revelation unveils to the church that God seeks to use us as witnesses to others so that we shine our light brightly and stand firm against the rulers of the day, even as the church in many places is presently suffering. Why? Because Jesus, and not Caesar (nor any government or political leader today), is Lord of the world. God's judgement on the world's rulers and

---

19. So Gorman, *Becoming the Gospel*, 19.

evildoers will come, and then he will usher in his new age of the kingdom in which his faithful people will be privileged to enter.

The most amazing news of all is this: *God has already written the end of his story*. God has spoken and so it will happen. And he has written this end to his story in *vision form*, to enlarge our imaginations, to attract us to the future, to invite us to move forward with him, to inspire us to live fully as his people. This vision, with its beauty, breadth and magnitude, should direct and shape our mission now. So let's turn to this vision.

God Makes a New Creation (Revelation 21–22)

Revelation 21–22 closes the canon with an immense crescendo:

> Then I saw "a new heaven and a new earth," for the first heaven and the first earth had passed away, and there was no longer any sea. I saw the Holy City, the new Jerusalem, coming down out of heaven from God, prepared as a bride beautifully dressed for her husband. And I heard a loud voice from the throne saying, "Look! God's dwelling-place is now among the people, and he will dwell with them. They will be his people, and God himself will be with them and be their God. 'He will wipe every tear from their eyes. There will be no more death' or mourning or crying or pain, for the old order of things has passed away."
>
> He who was seated on the throne said, "I am making everything new!" (Rev 21:1–5)

John sees a whole new creation! The Bible begins with creation and now ends with new creation. As you look into this vision of the new creation, you see that the end is so much grander than the beginning. The phrase "I saw 'a new heaven and a new earth'" picks up and fulfils the prophecy of Isaiah 65:17–25, and yet at the same time transcends it. Then there is the New Jerusalem, the Holy City, likened to the Holy of Holies, which later fills the earth. When it descends to earth, the wholeness of heavenly life comes down to humanity. *God's plan is not to take us to heaven, but to bring heaven to earth!* Next, a voice from heaven saying, "Behold, the tabernacle of God is among the people" (NASB) affirms that God has truly come to live with his *peoples* (plural)[20] on

---

20. The Greek, *laoi*, is plural, meaning "peoples," perhaps suggesting that the diversity of tribes and nations will not be obliterated in the new creation but somehow brought to a glorious and harmonious fulfilment.

the new earth (cf. Ezek 48:35). What was lost in the garden – unhindered fellowship with God – has now been regained. Because God is present with his people, there will be the complete wiping away of every tear as everything painful from the old order has gone.

And in verse 5 God himself now speaks and describes the new or second order. "Behold, I am making all things new. . . . Write, for these words are faithful and true" (NASB). God, the One on the throne, affirms what he is doing in his new creation. It is likely – and the word order ("I am making all things new" rather than "I am making all new things") may support this – that he is renewing *all* things: all that he intended for the original creation, which has been so ruined, is being restored so that it becomes all that he desires (cf. Rom 8:19–20).

In the next chapter, in Revelation 22:1–5, John sees

> the river of the water of life, as clear as crystal, flowing from the throne of God and of the Lamb down the middle of the great street of the city. On each side of the river stood the tree of life, bearing twelve crops of fruit, yielding its fruit every month. And the leaves of the tree are for the healing of the nations. No longer will there be any curse. The throne of God and of the Lamb will be in the city, and his servants will serve him. They will see his face, and his name will be on their foreheads. There will be no more night. They will not need the light of a lamp or the light of the sun, for the Lord God will give them light. And they will reign for ever and ever.

The New Jerusalem is described as the restoration of Eden which God's people can enjoy, experiencing fellowship with him and taking up their role of being priests and kings. We see the river of the water of life, irrigating the whole city. With the water flowing down the middle of the main street, this city is lush. Next, the tree of life reappears for the first time since Genesis 3, now bearing twelve crops of fruit, yielding its fruit *every month*. This is some orchard – amazing varieties of fruit, not once a year, but every month. And we hardly need to add that these will be the most delicious fruit ever tasted! We have abundant and life-giving food and drink in the new Eden. Even the leaves of the tree have a function: for the healing of the nations (cf. Ezek 47:12). We are seeing the redemption of the nations: life is flowing out as was the plan in Genesis 2. The curse of Genesis 3 is gone for ever (Rev 22:3)! Paradise Lost is now Paradise Regained.

John now comes to the ultimate blessing given to the redeemed humanity in the restored Eden: God himself is there with us, his people, for ever, *walking in his garden*. We will serve him, as originally called to do in the garden of Eden (Gen 2:15), now to be worked out in a much larger arena. We will enjoy a perfect relationship with God, since we will see his face, which for much of the Bible has been prohibited (Exod 33:20), and with his name on our foreheads we will be completely and eternally his. And if this were not enough, in his light, revelation and knowledge we will reign with God over the new creation for ever. In many ways the end is a new beginning. We are given the task of ruling over the new creation. This time we will not mess it up! New creation will blossom in its fullness.

This is truly an awesome conclusion to the vision. The beauty and harmony outlined in Genesis 1–2 is not only restored; it is developed and enhanced. Adam and Eve left a garden for a desert. Jesus is taking us from a desert to a garden city.

Contribution to Community Development

The end of the biblical story has an important role in guiding our community development efforts to a healthy destination, and I underscore the following points:

This is our vision. God has given this vision to us to shape our mission now. A full-orbed holistic vision of the future – integrating spirituality, physicality and community in a new creation – should give rise to a full-orbed holistic mission. If we lose sight of this vision, our imagination for community development in Africa will shrink, especially when trouble hits.

The character of the New Jerusalem should be employed to set the agenda for our mission. As Dean Flemming has shown by looking at the character of the New Jerusalem, mission should involve restored fellowship with God and others, a world-embracing, multi-ethnic, holy and healing community, the alleviation of pain and misery, social and economic justice (instead of the exploitation of "Babylon")[21] and the renewal of all creation.[22] Indeed, the picture

---

21. Babylon represents the city of Rome. In the Bible, Babylon often stands for the world against God, a dominant oppressive power that brings injustice and exploitation (e.g. Isa 47; Rev 17–18). God's people are to refuse to enter the *system* of Babylon, instead being a light-giving alternative.

22. Flemming, *Full Mission of God*, Kindle loc. 4171–216.

of the end is one of wholeness; harmony with God, ourselves, one another and the rest of creation.

God's future has already been launched. We are a new creation in Christ (2 Cor 5:17) – a preview of what God will do for the whole of creation later. So may the church in Africa be inspired to be a *signpost* and *instrument* to its communities of this future in Christ of a new creation. As God's people we have this secure hope of the future as we face trials and suffering now. Holding on to this vision and embracing the suffering that comes our way is all part of our faithful witness to others. And because of this hope, the church can always give itself fully to the Lord's work, including his work of community development, because its labour in the Lord is not in vain (1 Cor 15:58).

Reflections

As we come to the end of our journey through this grand story of the Bible, having seen the breadth of God's mission, there are two questions I wish to consider. First, where are we now in this story? And second, what vision of community does this story stimulate? To answer the first, we are in the fifth chapter, *the church*. This means that we, the church, are a key actor in the present stage of the story as we submit to Christ and are animated by the Spirit. God, in his wisdom, has always chosen to work *through a people* (Gen 1; 12; Exod 19; Luke 24) and it is our turn now. The resurrection of Jesus and the power of the Spirit propel us into our role in God's mission as we go with the secure hope and vision of the new creation to inspire us.

In answering the second question, we can say that the story advocates for this kind of community: a God-focused, vibrant, liberated, secure, healthy, hopeful, united, wise, inspired community where Jesus is Lord and which is marked by preferring others, righteousness, care of the needy, opportunity for all, love for the outsider, and enjoying and caring for its beautiful and fertile environment. This is what African communities are yearning for!

Therefore, may the people of God allow the whole biblical narrative to be their story as they work in partnership with God and engage their communities to see his kingdom and temple fill the world, where these communities increasingly enjoy his designs for life and worship him alone.

4

African, Western and Biblical Worldviews

Introduction

It is easier to articulate a vision for integral mission and community development than it is to implement one! Indeed, the world of praxis is fraught with all kinds of pitfalls, so much so that if we are not careful the vision is inadvertently cast aside and pragmatism takes over with huge loss for the church and communities. The rest of this book, therefore, is about working practically towards *allowing this grand biblical story to be the governing story of our life, work and mission, so that we move towards seeing this vision of thriving communities enjoying God and his goodness come to fruition.*

One of the fundamental issues to consider in working out this vision is how African and Western ways of thinking, acting and looking at the world are different. The responses of world leaders to the coronavirus pandemic illustrate the point beautifully. Whereas Western leaders tended to react to the crisis by seeking to control the spread of the virus and hence fix the problem, some African leaders responded differently, as seen, for example, in President Uhuru Kenyatta's more nuanced announcement when calling on Kenyans to pray:

> But fellow Kenyans even with these efforts [introduced measures], we cannot ignore the need to turn to God. In these circumstances as we have done in the past as a nation, we have always turned to God first to give thanks for the many blessings that He has bestowed on our nation. But we also turn to God to share our fears, our apprehensions, but also to seek his guidance and ever-present protection.

> We acknowledge always that we are nothing without our God.
>
> . . .
>
> On that day [the announced National Day of Prayer], through our religious leaders, we will be asking God for His forgiveness for anything that we may have done wrong or [that has] wronged Him.[1]

Why is this? Because their outlooks on life are different, causing them to act differently. One could not imagine a Western leader saying those words publicly.[2] Surely an acknowledgement of God's supremacy *and* seeking a proper and wise practical and medical response under his guidance is likely to be the best course of action faced with the coronavirus.

For those who work in integral mission and community development in Africa, there is often a clash of worldviews (which I will outline in a moment), leading to frustration and disappointment. This of course can happen between Westerners and their African colleagues and project participants. But since much funding for development comes from the West, even African development practitioners can feel the squeeze as they attempt to live between two cultures and two expectations. The biggest challenge we face in a clash of worldviews is that we are often neither aware of our own worldview and its implicit assumptions nor sufficiently appreciative of and acquainted with the other person's worldview.

The aim of this chapter is twofold. First, we will outline the way worldviews work, touch briefly on a Western worldview and some of its unhelpful features when it comes to development work in Africa, before considering some of the facets of a basic African worldview,[3] so that practitioners can think through a community development approach appropriate to their own African situation. And second, because all worldviews (African, Asian, South American and Western) are ultimately fallen and deficient, we will give practitioners the tools to consider how a biblical worldview and biblical understanding of poverty

---

1. "Proclamation of the National Day of Prayer by H. E. Uhuru Kenyatta, C.G.H., President of the Republic of Kenya and Commander-in-Chief of the Defence Forces, 17th March 2020," President of the Republic of Kenya, https://www.president.go.ke/2020/03/17/proclamation-of-the-national-day-of-prayer-by-h-e-uhuru-kenyatta-c-g-h-president-of-the-republic-of-kenya-and-commander-in-chief-of-the-defence-forces-17th-march-2020/?fbclid=IwAR1Q4x6_5abq SG6NWuIc6iH35CO7dbAXP4zETp7itgE3UyiD7qVEWu-WL3o.

2. The British prime minister Tony Blair, having wanted to encourage the public by concluding a speech with "God be with you," was told by an adviser, "We don't do God!"

3. Although Africa is a vast continent with many tribes and peoples, experts tend to believe there is enough commonality among them that it is possible to speak of an "African worldview" (e.g. Mburu, *African Hermeneutics*, 35).

impinge on and connect with an African worldview and African understanding of poverty so that the integral mission implemented brings healing and a deeper and lasting transformation.

What Is a Worldview?

When we come to consider what a worldview is we see that people tend to define it slightly differently, such as "a philosophy of life" or "a set of beliefs about the way things are." But I will use the term "worldview" to mean *the grid through which human beings perceive reality*. As N. T. Wright has shown, worldviews do four things:

> First, [they] provide the *stories* through which human beings view reality. . . . Second, from these stories one can in principle discover how to answer the basic *questions* that determine human existence: who are we, where are we, what is wrong, and what is the solution? . . . Third, the stories that express the worldview, and the answers which it provides to the questions of identity, environment, evil and eschatology, are expressed . . . in cultural *symbols*. . . . Fourth, worldviews include a praxis, a way-of-being-in-the-world. The implied eschatology of the fourth question ("what is the solution?") necessarily entails *action*.[4]

Every community, tribe or people has a worldview, whether they are conscious of it or not. It is basic to who they are and determines the way they approach life. As the description above shows, stories are fundamental to worldviews since stories give rise to them. The Western story differs considerably from African stories told from generation to generation; hence their worldviews are different, though with globalization these worldviews are beginning to move closer to one another. And this leads to an important point: worldviews are not static since the stories are still unfolding. For instance, people living in a village in Northern Uganda will have a quite different story from people who have grown up and are living in the rapidly changing city of Kampala.

---

4. N. T. Wright, *The New Testament and the People of God* (Minneapolis: Fortress, 1992), 122. Wright later added a fifth question, "What time is it?" (e.g. N. T. Wright, *Paul and the Faithfulness of God* [Minneapolis: Fortress, 2013], 550), which we can cover in a different way with the "now" and "not yet" of the kingdom of God.

The Unhelpfulness of the Western Worldview

"You have a very mechanical view of the world, but it doesn't work that way here," answered my Swahili teacher, Ishmael, in response to my question about how he saw us missionaries. Learning Swahili for five and a half hours a day straight was hard work, so we often paused to discuss Tanzanian culture and attitudes to life. Ishmael's reply was insightful, but I have to say that it took me years to dissect his wisdom here. My Muslim teacher went on to illustrate his point by explaining, "When you have an evangelistic outreach meeting, and you see the many people who have turned up, you exclaim, 'Wow, this place has found God!' But that's not necessarily true. Maybe they only came because they had nothing else to do or they thought you were going to give them a gift." Ishmael continued, "And if you see something different from you in people's life or behaviour, you just try to work out the reason in your own minds. But it's better to ask people questions to understand the values that give rise to the behaviour. So when you see us arriving late for your meeting, you just conclude that we don't understand time. But what you don't realize is that for us the most important thing is relationship, so if we meet a neighbour or friend on the way, we are going to talk to them, and if they require our help, then naturally we help them first." I think Ishmael hit the nail on the head! And as I began my time in Africa, he had given me invaluable advice that I would return to again and again.

It may be helpful briefly to summarize a Western worldview here. In a nutshell, since the Enlightenment, the dominant story of Western culture has been that through our reason, our knowledge, we can build a perfect world. The subtext is that we can do this *without God*, who is deemed irrelevant to the world. This anthropocentric story is called humanism. Progress, often aided through its associates science and technology, drives the story in which human beings are supposed to have dominion over the world. A high value is placed on rational thinking,[5] what is material over the immaterial, what is scientifically observable and what is objective. The focus is on the individual and on the individual taking his or her responsibility. The problem with the world, according to this worldview, is that people are not thinking rationally and thus solutions tend to focus on remedying this problem.

Although this worldview has faced many challenges over recent years with its deficiencies and flaws exposed, causing it to evolve to some degree, it is not hard to see how this worldview has been pre-eminent in development practice in Africa, such as with the phrase "Time is money," meaning the requirement

---

5. Although ironically there is much that is irrational in Western thinking!

to finish the job as quickly as possible. But this worldview has not served the African peoples well. And it is not all it is cracked up to be. Indeed, one bishop's wife, who had spent considerable time in the UK gaining a PhD there, said to me, "I like living here in Africa. Life has more meaning."

An African Worldview

In this section, I give some basic orientation to an African worldview, drawing out features that are commonly present in the thoughts of many African peoples. It is best for you the reader to use this section as just a starting point, and then to do two things. First, utilize good resources to discover more.[6] And second, spend intentional time with the particular people or tribe you are working with to understand their worldview better and to hear their story.

African Stories of the World

As I mentioned at the beginning of this chapter, people's stories both express their worldview and are provided by their worldview. So let us look at one example of an African people's story. The Pangwa people, close to the shores of Lake Malawi in Njombe, Southern Tanzania, have their own story of creation.[7]

> Before there was a sun, a moon, or stars, there was only wind and a tree where some ants lived. There was also the Word, which controlled everything, but could not be seen. The Word was a catalyst for creation.
>
> Once the wind became angry at the tree for standing in its way, so it blew particularly hard, tearing off a branch on which there were white ants. When they landed, the ants were hungry, so they ate all of the leaves on the branch, sparing only one, on which they defecated a huge pile.
>
> Then they had no choice but to eat their own excrement, and over time, as they ate and redeposited their excrement, the pile became a mountain that finally spread to the original tree. By then

---

6. E.g. Mburu, *African Hermeneutics*, in chapters 2–4 has an up-to-date discussion on the African worldview and how it is changing as well as giving a helpful bibliography.

7. Taken from David A. Leeming, *Creation Myths of the World: An Encyclopedia*, vol. 1, 2nd ed. (Santa Barbara: ABC-Clio, 2010), 273–74. Healey and Sybertz, *African Narrative Theology*, 62–64, also document some African creation stories with insightful consequences.

the ants preferred excrement to leaves, and they continued the process of adding to the pile until it became the earth.

The wind still blew on the world so strongly that parts of the excrement pile began to harden into stone. The world gradually formed, until the Word sent snow and then warm wind, which melted the snow and brought a huge flood. The waters killed the ants; there was water covering everything.

Later the earth and the world tree joined, and the trees, grasses, rivers, and oceans took form. The air gave birth to beings that flew about singing. These beings came to Earth and became animals, birds, and humans, each with its own song or language.

The new beings were hungry. The animals wanted to eat the Tree of Life, but the humans defended it. This led to a huge war between humans and animals, and to the tradition of humans and animals eating each other. The war was so ferocious that the earth shook, and bits and pieces of it flew off, gained heat, and became the sun, moon, and stars.

After the war there was the creation of gods, rain, thunder, and lightning. A long-tailed sheep with a single horn was so happy at the end of the great war that she leapt into the air, caught fire, and became the source of thunder and lightning.

The new gods who sprang up were harsh with humans. One of them told the people that the sheep that had sprung into the air had killed the Word, the ultimate creator, and that the people would be reduced in size and in the end would be consumed by fire.

Although we may see some superficial similarities with the biblical story, not least in the Word (which incidentally does not become flesh), the Tree of Life and a flood, this story is a sad story, as it explains how the world came to be in the state it is, with little hope of salvation. The world has little purpose (being created chaotically), a lack of peace from the beginning, and there appears no understanding of who human beings are, nor of their role in the world. Moreover, the creator Word, who is not a true creator but just a catalyst with much creation occurring through lesser gods, has no relationship with humans and ultimately becomes killed himself.

Although there are many variations in African creation stories and stories of the world, as you would expect, typically they tell of the world being made by one God, who can sometimes but not always be assisted by lesser divinities, and this God will often withdraw at some point from his creation. Humans are not created to be anything special, nor are they assigned any role in the world.[8] Often, once rebellion has taken place or evil has come in the world, there is the sense that humans have to continue to live out their days under the consequences of evil with no hope of redemption.[9] There is no evidence of any future hope of living in a perfected state.[10] Indeed, there is no sense that this world is going anywhere. The best that people can hope for in life is to live in harmony with the spirit world, their community and nature. For average village farmers this means that what they can hope for will be simply to have enough to get by in life.

Pertinent Characteristics of a Traditional African Worldview

In order to delve a little more deeply into understanding the traditional African worldview, it is helpful to describe its salient characteristics or features. We begin with the most important.

Supreme Being. In almost all African stories and religions there is a Supreme Being, the God above all other spiritual beings, who created the world and everything in it. After his work of creation is completed or because of human transgression, he often withdraws and his involvement in the world generally stops or reduces.[11] Though great and powerful, this Being is commonly seen as remote or unapproachable directly by humans.[12] The Supreme Being is usually seen as ultimately responsible for everything that happens in the world, as nothing can happen without him, but at the same time he is never blamed for evil.[13] It is thus completely logical that African leaders, speaking to and on behalf of people in this story, would immediately turn to God in

---

8. I have not come across anything remotely close to this understanding in any account.

9. E.g. see Kathryn McClymond, Julius H. Bailey, Robert André LaFleur and Grant L. Voth, *Great Mythologies of the World* (Chantilly: The Teaching Company, 2015), 173–249, whose extensive survey of African stories and their components shows no hope of redemption.

10. John Mbiti, "God, Sin, and Salvation in African Religion," *The Journal of the Interdenominational Theological Center* 16, no. 1–2 (Fall 1988–Spring 1989): 63.

11. See Samuel Waje Kunhiyop, *African Christian Theology* (Grand Rapids: Zondervan Academic, 2012), Kindle loc. 1473.

12. See Rodney Reed and Gift Mtukwa, "Christ Our Ancestor: African Christology and the Danger of Contextualization," *Wesleyan Theological Journal* 45, no. 1 (Spring 2010): 149; and Chigoe Chike, "Proudly African, Proudly Christian: The Roots of Christologies in the African Worldview," *Black Theology* 6, no. 2 (May 2008): 223.

13. P. Yakubu Otijele, "Understanding the African Worldview: A Religious Perspective," *Ogbomoso Journal of Theology* (6 Dec. 1991): 11.

the coronavirus pandemic.[14] Africans do however tend to interact with God in a transactional rather than a relational way,[15] an approach often carried over when they become Christians. So is the Supreme Being identical to the God of the Bible? While we may be tempted to say "Yes" with John Mbiti,[16] as Mburu says, "the God of the Bible is clearly superior,"[17] both in his character and in his coming to us.[18]

Divinities and spirits. These lesser spiritual beings often take on the running of the world, assisting the Supreme Being, and may have different areas of influence (e.g. wind, sea, fertility). These spiritual beings, along with the ancestors, "figure very prominently in the traditional African worldview"[19] and they are deeply revered since they are intermediaries to the Supreme Being.[20] Communities often offer prayers to the Supreme Being through these intermediaries.

Ancestors. When community members die, they can continue as community members, becoming the "living dead," assisting the above group of spiritual beings. Not everyone qualifies to be an ancestor but only those who have lived a moral life and served their community well. These ancestors have tremendous access into the world of spirits which govern the earth and the ancestors can either bless or curse the community. I have heard of people saying that their day is not going well because their (deceased) grandmother is angry. Communities, thus living in fear of these spiritual powers and ancestors, seek to please them so that their ancestors may continue to act for them – otherwise these ancestors may act against them in their influence with the spiritual powers. Intrinsically connected to this is often the belief in witchcraft in which a person may visit a diviner as a way to gain favourable access with such powers and spirits.[21]

---

14. Mbiti, "God, Sin, and Salvation," who notes, "If the community itself experiences misfortunes like epidemics, locust invasion, drought, disastrous flooding or famine, it was customary in most societies to seek help from God" (65).

15. Mburu, *African Hermeneutics*, 38.

16. Mbiti, "God, Sin, and Salvation," 61.

17. Mburu, *African Hermeneutics*, 37.

18. This coming to us occurs throughout the Bible and supremely in Jesus.

19. Reed and Mtukwa, "Christ Our Ancestor," 148.

20. Chike, "Roots of Christologies," 223.

21. Monger and Methuselah, "God's Masterpiece," 105.

Human beings. As mentioned above, there appears to be no sense in African traditional thinking that human beings are significant[22] or have a particular role or responsibility in the world as we saw in Genesis 1.[23] There seems no expectation of human beings to work in partnership with God to develop the world. Creation stories tend simply to state that human beings are created, along with the animals, and offer a description of how the world "went wrong" and a reason for the way human beings find it as they do. With an overriding appreciation of the Supreme Being's full control of the world, Africans can sometimes appear to those from the West as fatalistic and lacking the desire to take responsibility.

Community. Africans are profoundly community people. As Mbiti so famously said, "I am because we are and since we are, therefore I am,"[24] which is in contradistinction to the Western individualistic view expressed by Descartes, "I think, therefore I am." In Africa "the individual does not exist except in the life of the concrete community. Without the community, the individual has no life and no meaning."[25] To Africans, their family and community matter deeply to them, and they put themselves out for the benefit of others. They concentrate on maintaining the community and in fact get their identity from their community. Doing things for the community is second nature since relationships bring life and people suffer and rejoice together. In this way, if relationships are damaged, Africans will often do their utmost to restore them, even at personal cost, since to be "ostracized from the community is the most severe of all punishment in many African societies – it can be tantamount to death."[26]

Holistic view of life. Everything is created by the one God and nothing happens outside of his will. The universe is a spiritual universe and hence all of life is seen as sacred.[27] There is no material/physical world and then a spiritual world; rather the two are interconnected and impact one another.[28] So the rains may fail because the ancestors are displeased. Life is to be lived in harmony

---

22. There is often a lack of belief that human life has intrinsic value, as seen for example in the absence of concern for health and safety.

23. Surprisingly, Kunhiyop, *African Christian Theology*, makes no attempt to connect the creation of humanity in God's image in Genesis 1 to African views of personhood.

24. John Mbiti, *African Religions and Philosophy*, 2nd ed. (Oxford: Heinemann, 1989), 106.

25. Reed and Mtukwa, "Christ Our Ancestor," 147.

26. Chike, "Roots of Christologies," 224.

27. Chike, 222.

28. Mburu notes, "Africans assume that God, the spirits, ancestors, human beings, and objects all inhabit one world" (*African Hermeneutics*), 42–43.

with the community, the spiritual beings and nature, as together they form an interconnected whole. Again, this is different from a Western way of thinking which is dualistic, separating the physical/material and spiritual into distinct spheres, where the lack of rain can be explained in purely physical terms. But not so in Africa, nor in the Bible!

Sin. As human beings are people in relationships, sin is primarily seen as that which disturbs the harmony of those relationships, whether in the community or with spirits and ancestors or even with nature.[29] In this way, the effect of sin is seen holistically.[30] This is different from a Western understanding of sin which focuses on an individual's transgression of the law and therefore holds that individual guilty. African societies, instead of being innocence-guilt based, tend to be more honour-shame based, whereby the sin, by bringing disharmony to relationships, results in shame and the loss of honour for community members. The restoration of honour is required by the person who sinned. When a sin is committed, the community will require the person to make amends through such things as sacrifices to the ancestors by slaughtering animals.[31] Sin is very much a present life issue which must be sorted out in the present. The desire for forgiveness is not for the removal of guilt but so that the person may be able to have access to a good and successful life.

Salvation. In Africa, people will tend to desire and pray for what we might call the "good life," a life in the present which includes provision of life, health, children, success, a harvest, good standing in the community, and protection against the powers and forces that prevent such a life.[32] With a holistic view of life and belief that God controls all things, it is not surprising that many Africans see transformation holistically, touching the whole of their lives. The so-called "spiritual" salvation of the West, which leaves unaltered the physical and communal aspects of people's lives, does not connect well with African peoples. The Almighty God is expected to do more! As Osadolor Imasogi says, "Christ must be proclaimed as the cosmic Lord who is more than able to supply all human needs. . . . Christ's saving concern must be seen as transcending

---

29. Mbiti, "God, Sin, and Salvation," 65.

30. Charles Nyamiti, "Contemporary Liberation Theologies in the Light of the African Traditional Conception of Evil," *Studia Missionalia* 45 (1996): 242, who notes that it affects (1) life, resulting in weakness, (2) communal and cosmic dimensions, (3) the religious dimension and (4) human welfare.

31. Mbiti, "God, Sin, and Salvation," 65; Reed and Mtukwa, "Christ Our Ancestor," 151.

32. Chike, "Roots of Christologies," 226 and 232; and Mbiti, 66.

narrow spiritual salvation to include liberation from human oppression and the reconciliation of man to God, to fellow humans, and to nature."[33]

Time. Africans traditionally do not have a concept of time as a linear phenomenon; rather it is considered to be cyclical.[34] In biblical thinking, which has also impacted the Western concept of time, time is linear, moving from the past to the present and on to the future; thus it is a commodity to be valued and used wisely (Ps 90:10–12). But in African thinking, since time is cyclical, one expects to see the current opportunity again and so there may be no pressing need to do something now. My Tanzanian colleagues often seek to explain to villagers that this is not necessarily the case and that, for example, seasonal activities need to be done "on time." Generally speaking, Africans view time in terms of events "stretching from the past into the present but not going far into the future."[35] The question whether Africans lack a sense of the future is a moot point.[36] But what we can definitely say is that there is an understanding of the past, present and immediate future,[37] but the distant future is less clear. This discussion on time, coupled with the relational view of life described above, is highly significant in terms of undertaking community development activities, particularly in planning matters and fulfilling priorities. Africans and Westerners working together in projects need to appreciate one another's viewpoints here or there may be friction and frustration.[38]

These are some of the basic characteristics of a traditional African worldview. Although this worldview is dynamic and changing through the influence of other worldviews, and many African pastors and development workers may not share this worldview and story entirely, either through their upbringing or training, it is vital that they appreciate and become acquainted with it, thinking through step by step how it impinges on community development.

---

33. Osadolor Imasogi, "The Church and Theological Ferment in Africa," *Review & Expositor* 82, no. 2 (Spring 1985): 228.

34. So Chike, "Roots of Christologies," 225.

35. Chike, 225; and Ogbu U. Kalu, "Preserving a Worldview: Pentecostalism in the African Maps of the Universe," *Pneuma: The Journal of the Society for Pentecostal Studies* 24, no. 2 (Fall 2002): 119.

36. Chike, "Roots of Christologies," 225.

37. The immediate future is appreciated because they are aware of events that customarily happen and thus can be expected to come again (e.g. school days and Sunday church services).

38. The Western viewpoint tends to be task- and time-driven whereas the African tends to be people-centred.

The African Story Continued: Emerging from Colonialization

It goes without saying that the colonial era has had a profound influence on the African worldview, even as traditional characteristics retain a significant place in it. The colonial era has brought tremendous pain, oppression, exploitation, and much damage to people's identity. Westerners frequently do not appreciate the extent of the injuries caused by colonialization, which has set back the chance for Africa to lead its own development.

The last sixty years or so have seen much of Africa struggling to emerge from this colonial period. The struggle for independence has not led into a period of blessing for the peoples of Africa for at least a couple of noteworthy reasons. First, the world that independent Africa has come into is not a just world with a level playing field. On the contrary, the Western and former colonial powers still hold the upper hand and unfair advantage, displayed even today in such things as increasing interest payments on the debt of many low-income African countries, the heavy effect on Africa of the climate crisis and the shortage of COVID-19 vaccinations for African nations. And second, as Emmanuel Katongole has highlighted in his insightful book *The Sacrifice of Africa*,[39] many of Africa's leaders have in effect sadly continued the colonial story by ruling for themselves and not for their people.[40] According to Katongole, the focus of African leaders has tended to be on holding on to power rather than on equitable nation-building.[41] There has been "the sacrificing of Africa" through their greed, ambition and oppressive regimes.[42] These leaders have often perpetuated tribalism and the resultant violence and poverty, and offered a vision of "mere survival" to their peoples.[43] It is not a story that inspires hope and change. Today, there are also the stories of globalization and the prosperity gospel nestling in on Africa's stories, and holding out false hope.

What should be obvious is that Africa needs a new, liberating and revitalizing story in which Africans can live. What Katongole and I are arguing for in our own ways is that the church, by living God's story and taking the nature of a servant, is uniquely placed to supply this life-giving story, which

---

39. Emmanuel Katongole, *The Sacrifice of Africa: A Political Theology for Africa* (Grand Rapids, MI: Eerdmans, 2011).

40. Katongole, *Sacrifice of Africa*, 73–74.

41. Katongole, 73.

42. Katongole, 15–17.

43. Katongole, 79.

connects to and heals the pain of existing stories, and imagines a new future.[44] As the church reflects on the way it has often conducted itself and its ministry, *it should be apparent that in many places a Christian veneer has simply been laid over the traditional belief system and ways of thinking since independence, which explains why Christianity has not developed deeper roots and brought a deeper and wider transformation.*

A contextual approach is what is required, whereby the church and its workers, shaped by a biblical worldview and animated by the life of the Spirit, engage fully with the local culture, knowing which elements are avenues for the good news, which elements need to be reworked and which elements simply need to be confronted, as we see, for instance, with Paul in Athens (Acts 17:16–34). In this way, the community will be drawn into God's story, having their story and worldview healed and reworked so they enjoy his life. With this in mind, I now sum up a biblical worldview and the framework it gives us.

A Biblical Worldview

The Bible as story gives rise to a worldview. That is why we spent the last two chapters surveying the biblical story and its contribution to integral mission and community development, *so we move towards a biblical worldview, living out God's story, rather than trying to superimpose on others our broken, incomplete and ineffectual stories.* I will be utilizing the contributions we saw in the biblical story in the coming chapters as we consider the outworking of this vision of integral mission and community development in an African context. The biblical story answers the fundamental questions of our lives as Christians: *Who are we? Where are we? What is the problem?* and *What is the solution?* I briefly outline the answers to those questions now:

Who are we? We are people made in the image of God and being remade in Jesus to be the community of God, transcending old tribal distinctions, and called to rule wisely in the world under our King and spreading his transforming kingship.

Where are we? We are in God's good creation, which though marred by the fall is sustained by him and lovingly being made new again.

---

44. Katongole, 84. I only came across Katongole's *Sacrifice of Africa* as I was finishing the manuscript of this book, but I was heartened to discover that he argues that the church can interrupt and transform the status quo and create a different and better story for Africa.

What is the problem? We, human beings, have rebelled against the Creator God and fractured the world, bringing evil, pain, injustice, poverty and the loss of harmonious relationships.

What is the solution? The Creator God responded in calling Abraham and Israel and has come himself in Jesus to fulfil Old Testament promises by giving a death blow to evil and establishing his kingdom to set the world right. This task is being carried forward by his people, the church, through the power of the Spirit, announcing this good news of Jesus in being, word and deed to every community so they too can join God's people as God brings his world to his intended glorious goal where he will be all in all.

So, by being shaped by this biblical worldview, we are given the right glasses needed to participate with God in the most expansive and exciting community development work and see the poor enjoying the good news of God. It is time now to go a step further and consider how these African and biblical worldviews understand poverty, for without doing so we may bring our assumptions to bear uncritically and communities will miss out on God's larger transformation.

The Perspective on Poverty in Africa and the Bible
Poverty in Africa

Poverty in Africa is a huge topic with multiple viewpoints regarding what it actually is. Its existence is the context which has given rise to the current book. It is vital to have a good understanding of the nature and shape of poverty in Africa and to infuse that with an appreciation of what the Bible says about poverty in order to assist the church to know how to respond appropriately. Sadly, typical poverty alleviation efforts are a prime example of Western approaches and assumptions that have often failed Africa, either by misconstruing poverty or by treating the presenting issues or symptoms rather than the underlying causes. However, there are some excellent resources, books and articles on understanding poverty in both Africa and the Bible, and I advise you to read them to appreciate the significance of poverty. Here I mention three particular resources. Bryant Myers, *Walking with the Poor*,[45] and Steve Corbett and Brian Fikkert, *When Helping Hurts*,[46] both include a good discussion on

---

45. Bryant L. Myers, *Walking with the Poor: Principles and Practices of Transformational Development*, rev. and expanded ed. (Maryknoll: Orbis, 2011).

46. Steve Corbett and Brian Fikkert, *When Helping Hurts: How to Alleviate Poverty without Hurting the Poor . . . and Yourself*, 2nd ed. (Chicago: Moody, 2012).

poverty from a biblical point of view as well as some cultural analysis. However, they do not deal specifically with Africa. In particular, Myers draws on the work of Jayakumar Christian who writes in and to an Indian context. The third resource is *Poverty, the Bible, and Africa* by Isaac Boaheng,[47] who writes as an African with Africa in mind.

Poverty is a multifaceted phenomenon and there are many ways it could be analysed.[48] My aim here is to outline poverty in Africa sufficiently so we understand its interconnecting dimensions.

Lack of basic necessities. The most obvious dimension of poverty is the lack of basic necessities, such as water, food, clothing, shelter and sanitation. Without these things, people struggle physically to live. Individuals and families have few material possessions and often lack sufficient land to provide for themselves. They and their children often lack health and education, which are also basic necessities, and the cycle of poverty continues. This dimension of poverty therefore also relates to the economic situation. Many times, we as both Africans and Westerners can fail to see beyond this dimension, thinking it is all that there is. But equally, we must never overlook this fundamental dimension and should consider an appropriate response for its long-term alleviation.

Social exclusion. The second dimension is social exclusion. The poor suffer in their relationships with the community, which may be an outflow of their lack of basic necessities. They may be excluded or rejected by others. Their views may be dismissed by others. Because of the African worldview, Boaheng says, "an African needs to feel part of, and be accepted by, the community because his or her existence depends more on community support than individualism."[49] It is therefore not enough to consider only the lack of basic necessities; the church must also think about restoring people's relationships with their community. After all, a life without friendship is very poor indeed.

Powerlessness. Third, being poor often includes having one's rights denied and a powerlessness to gain access to these rights, and consequently to have the chance to succeed in life. Such people can be extremely vulnerable to exploitation, with others taking advantage of them. The widow may lose the family's land and hence the ability to provide for herself. The poor are often

---

47. Isaac Boaheng, *Poverty, the Bible, and Africa: Contextual Foundations for Helping the Poor* (Carlisle: HippoBooks, 2020).

48. As Myers wisely says, "I doubt there is or ever will be a unified theory of poverty. There is always more to see and more to learn. The corrective is to keep using a family of views to see all the things we need to see. We must work hard to be as holistic as we can be for the sake of the poor" (*Walking with the Poor*, 132–33).

49. Boaheng, *Poverty, the Bible, and Africa*, Kindle loc. 604.

voiceless, meaning their cries are not heard or listened to by those in power. They are considered to be less significant. Many Christians and others advocate for the poor to ensure they gain justice and receive their rights as human beings.

Dehumanization. Poverty is immensely dehumanizing. This dimension connects with the previous one but goes much deeper. Boaheng says, "The poor in most African societies are not respected; they are insulted and not taken seriously. They are vulnerable and objects of exploitation and injustice."[50] The poor often feel shame about who they are and the state of their lives. Their children are ridiculed at school. The father is unable to hold his head up high since he is bowed down with humiliation and failure. Sometimes people talk in this regard about a *poverty of being*. This is reflected in a lack of confidence, feelings of inadequacy and shame, and a lack of any hope that things could be different. I should point out that colonization has contributed to this aspect of poverty, in that the former colonial powers as they expressed their dominance conveyed their own superiority and the African people's inferiority. Even today, the tragic effects of this part of Africa's story are still seen in the damage done to the identities of communities in Africa.

Spiritual poverty. Fifth, some experts include the category of being spiritually poor, although in many ways this category is a part of being dehumanized or of a poverty of being. Africa is an immensely spiritual continent and for many there is a sense that the spirit world is against them. As Myers says, "The household suffers from broken and dysfunctional relationships with God, each other, the community, and creation. Its members may suffer from spiritual oppression in the form of fear of spirits, demons, and angry ancestors. They may lack hope and be unable to believe that change is possible."[51] At the same time, sometimes the materially poor are spiritually rich as they have learned to depend on God as their provider (Luke 6:20). It is vital that in any of our efforts to assist the poor to alleviate their poverty we do not undercut their dependency on God. Furthermore, it is important that we all realize that at some level we are all poor, so that we interact as equals with communities, learn from them and all experience God's healing of our identities.

As we work in poor communities, it is vital we appreciate all these dimensions and how they interlock, while recognizing that they will be expressed differently in each place and community.

---

50. Boaheng, Kindle loc. 622.
51. Myers, *Walking with the Poor*, 115.

Poverty in the Bible

The poor in the Bible are often described in socio-economic or political terms and their plight and afflictions are described vividly.[52] Even though the Mosaic law calls Israel to treat the poor rightly, whether they be brothers and sisters or foreigners (Exod 22:21; Lev 25:35; Deut 15:7–11), the poor are frequently the victims of greed, exploitation and abuse of power, as we saw in Amos. And a poor person will be shunned by his or her friends and neighbours and will experience humiliation (Prov 14:20). Sadly, the poor are seen as having no one to turn to except God, who "is portrayed as One who responds to the cries of the poor, especially the needy among his people."[53] As we saw, Jesus, as God's Son, shapes his ministry as good news to the poor, liberating them from their oppression (Luke 4:18–21). The Epistles recognize the bleak plight of the poor who lack "food, clothes or decent wages (Jas 2:1–19; 5:1–6)."[54] At the same time, poverty can lead to a healthy dependence on God as provider, and we often see the poor responding to the gospel message.

The solution to poverty in both Testaments is based on recognizing a *communal mindset in right relationship to God*, so that the people of God should ensure there is righteousness in community living, treating the poor as family members, both providing generously for them and working for their justice. Equally, each person is expected to work hard to provide for his or her own needs and not simply rely on others (1 Thess 4:11; 2 Thess 3:6–10). Laziness brings poverty (Prov 10:4). Finally, God is displayed throughout the Bible as being on the side of the poor and he calls his people to take up this concern (Ps 140:12).

Conclusions on Poverty in Africa and the Bible

We see here that the pictures of poverty in Africa and in the Bible are similar, with the dimensions of African poverty being found also in the Bible. In both African and biblical viewpoints, poverty is all-embracing, with material, social, economic, political and spiritual aspects. If we ask the question "Does poverty exist because people are broken or because systems are broken?," African and biblical perspectives agree that poverty is both personal and systemic. Broken

---

52. Leland Ryken et al., eds., *Dictionary of Biblical Imagery* (Downers Grove, IL: InterVarsity Press 1998), 657.

53. Ryken et al., *Dictionary of Biblical Imagery*, 658.

54. Ryken et al., 658.

people create broken systems that break others.[55] People experience poverty due to their own failings, such as in their lack of attentiveness in farming while their neighbour's field with similar soil is blooming. And they experience poverty because the system is against them, for instance when money allotted for their development is diverted by corrupt officials. Any attempt to deal with poverty that does not deal with both personal and systemic aspects is likely doomed to failure. The Bible however also recognizes that our sin contributes to our poverty (Deut 28:15–68). All of us, including the materially poor and the exploited, are sinners and our sins mar our identity, disabling us from thriving. So sensitively placing dealing with sin in the mix of our endeavours is essential to real poverty alleviation.

Most significantly, both African and biblical perspectives on poverty emphasize the *relational* dimensions of poverty. Poverty is essentially about broken relationships. God created each one of us for a relationship with him, with self (a proper understanding of who we are), with others (in our family, community and outside) and with the rest of creation. "These relationships are the building blocks for all of life."[56] But when they are not functioning correctly poverty ensues, as Myers articulates: "Poverty is a result of relationships that do not work, that are not just, that are not for life, that are not harmonious or enjoyable. Poverty is the absence of shalom in all its meanings."[57] This is not who we have been created to be as people in God's image. God's intent is that people live out their being in his image, knowing their God-worth, taking their place in the community and fulfilling "their callings of glorifying God by working and supporting themselves and their families with the fruit of that work"[58] as part of God's wider creational purposes. And both Boaheng[59] and the Bible[60] highlight the importance of the community taking initiative and just action to alleviate the poverty of those in their midst, an approach that I believe has been underemployed in Africa but should be included among efforts to see the poor lifted up and enjoying restored relationships.

Thankfully, as we have seen in chapters 2 and 3, the Bible shows the solution to poverty as the healing of *all* those relationships, a healing wrought in Jesus Christ and now carried forward justly and compassionately by the church as

---

55. So Corbett and Fikkert, *When Helping Hurts*, 147.
56. Corbett and Fikkert, 55.
57. Myers, *Walking with the Poor*, 143.
58. Corbett and Fikkert, *When Helping Hurts*, 57.
59. Boaheng, *Poverty, the Bible, and Africa*, Kindle loc. 3211.
60. E.g. Lev 25:35; Deut 15:7–11; Luke 11:39–46; Acts 2:44–45; 4:32–36; Gal 2:10; Jas 1:27.

it participates with him (the subject of the next chapter). This is beautifully seen, for example, in Colossians 1:15–20:

> The Son is the image of the invisible God, the firstborn over *all* creation. For in him *all* things were created: things in heaven and on earth, visible and invisible, whether thrones or powers or rulers or authorities; *all* things have been created through him and for him. He is before *all* things, and in him *all* things hold together. And he is the head of the body, the church; he is the beginning and the firstborn from among the dead, so that in *everything* he might have the supremacy. For God was pleased to have *all* his fullness dwell in him, and through him to reconcile to himself *all* things, whether things on earth or things in heaven, by making peace through his blood, shed on the cross. (Emphasis added.)

As the church participates with Christ by the Spirit in integral mission it will be able to show how those restored four fundamental relationships *intersect and facilitate a whole-life harmony*. For example, a restored relationship with God should lead to a healed view of oneself and hence to a renewed commitment to love one's neighbours and a constructive attitude to creation, which after all is God's world and shared with one's neighbours.

5

Working with the Church for Its Mission

Why Should the African Church Involve Itself in Development?

In chapter 1 we looked at the open door for the church in community development and poverty eradication in Africa. But just because there is an opportunity for the church, does that mean the church should take it? In this case, I would say yes, for two principal reasons. First, although much development in Africa has been done for many years by secular organizations, experts are increasingly seeing that faith-based organizations (FBOs), such as churches, have an important role in bringing development in the Majority World. Over a century ago Christians were at the forefront in seeking to raise the living standards within many African countries through, for instance, founding mission schools and hospitals. But after the Second World War, and as many African countries gained independence in the 1960s, the role of FBOs in the mainstream of development gradually waned as a secular approach took shape. In Tanzania, for example, even many mission schools were taken over and run by the government after independence and the church was left on the margins to concentrate on "spiritual" matters. Since the early 2000s, however, this consensus of a secular framework for development has begun to shift in practice.[1] Indeed, it has been acknowledged that "unless approaches

---

1. Emma Tomalin, "Religions, Poverty Reduction and Global Development Institutions," *Palgrave Communications* 4, Article 132 (2018): 1. "In February 1998 leaders of several world religions met at Lambeth Palace in London upon the invitation of the then Archbishop of Canterbury, George Carey, and James Wolfensohn, president of the World Bank. This meeting can be viewed as a sign of the reorientation which was about to take place in the relationship between international development actors and religious leaders. It implied a new understanding of religion and religious actors' role in development, and with it a growing interest in faith-based

to development are consistent with the inherited moral base of society, which is shaped by religion, they are likely to be ineffective."[2] This is not surprising, since as we saw in the previous chapter life in Africa is shaped by spiritual realities, so to ignore them is futile. The church is uniquely placed to offer real development to Africa's peoples. Nordstokke describes the value of FBOs in bringing significant change that other actors frequently lack, thus rendering their own efforts less effectual:

> FBOs are believed to have a particular expertise when it comes to addressing religious traditions and religion's role in promoting development. It is further presumed that their social character will keep them close to people at the grassroots level, making them able to communicate in a way that connects with people's basic worldview and values when they are involved in projects and programmes.[3]

While many development organizations operate "at a distance" from the target communities, with their employees spending much time working in town or city offices, the church is present with the community and has a great affinity with it, which results in the community more readily receiving the church's ideas and initiatives and partnering with it.

The second reason why the church should involve itself in development is because of the biblical mandate for the people of God to join him in bringing his transforming kingdom in every place and among every people, as we saw in chapters 2 and 3. In this light, development is interpreted as the growth of the kingdom of God and is integral to the church's mission. The story of the Bible told earlier, particularly through the theme of *kingdom*, could equally have been told through the theme of *peoplehood*. It is God's chosen way to use his people to bring his kingdom in the world. Initially, this was to be done through all humanity (Gen 1:26–27), but after humanity falls (Gen 3) he works through a particular people, Israel, as the channel of drawing all peoples to himself and revealing his kingdom purposes to them (Gen 12:1–3; Exod 19:5–6). Even though Israel as a whole fail, God comes himself in Jesus as a member of Israel to be the Saviour of the world (Matt 1:1; John 4:42). And now those who respond to Jesus, Jew and Gentile alike, become a people, the

---

organisations and their specific contribution" (Kjell Nordstokke, "Faith-Based Organisations [FBOs] and Their Distinct Assets," *Swedish Missiological Themes* 101, no. 2 [2013]: 186).

2. Tomalin, "Poverty Reduction," 5.

3. Nordstokke, "Faith-Based Organisations," 189.

church, the true children of Abraham, who are to be a light to the world (Matt 5:16; Gal 3:9). And at the end of time, this people reigns with God over the new creation (Rev 22:5).

With the enormity of the challenges in Africa, "it is obvious that only God through his power can renew all things,"[4] and he has chosen to work principally through his people, the church, which needs "constantly to view poverty as a scourge of human life, for the Bible condemns it as a scandalous condition demanding justice, and emphasises that God wants an end to it."[5]

So who is better placed to undertake and oversee real community development than the local church? *No other organization can hold out a full vision of a healthy and vibrant community.*[6] In this chapter, I examine the foundations of helping the church involve itself in the precious work of Christian community development.

Preliminaries in Setting up Church-Based Community Development

Working in community development to change lives can be so exciting that it is easy to rush quickly into things and forget to think through the issues sufficiently and set up matters properly. For some of us, we just have the desire to "get going"! The mission student fresh out of seminary or the pastor back from an inspiring conference is eager to get stuck in. And the expatriate missionary, having spent months learning the local language, cannot wait any longer. But taking time to think through the issues can pay huge dividends in the long run. It is like being in the bustling Ubungo bus stand in Dar es Salaam, Tanzania, and taking a few minutes to locate the right bus, check its destination stuck onto the windscreen, and not simply accept the view of a ticket seller. You can avoid finding yourself at the wrong end of the country after sleeping most of the journey!

In my time in Tanzania, I was privileged to work with churches of different denominations across the theological spectrum. There was one my organization had been in partnership with for over fifteen years before I arrived. But as time went on, we realized we were missing the point, and we began thinking how we could get things back on track. Although good efforts were happening in

---

4. Deborah Ajulu, "Development as Holistic Mission," in *Holistic Mission: God's Plan for God's People*, Edinburgh Centenary 5, eds. Brian Woolnough and Wonsuk Ma (Oxford: Regnum, 2010), 172.

5. Ajulu, "Development as Holistic Mission," 173.

6. Even Christian NGOs are often unable to push forward on all fronts through fear of being seen to proselytize.

localities on the ground and villagers were benefiting, we all knew that overall a deeper connection with the diocese was lacking. My colleagues searched hard but could not even find a memorandum of understanding (MOU) between us and the church. No wonder we had become the development arm of the church! Whether or not there was ever an agreed MOU, the fact is that it was not passed on to us. We lacked a shared vision and purpose. Our partnership had become misshapen, expectations were already fixed and approaches were set in their ways. As colleagues talked to the bishop, he could see and admitted that the partnership had got off course. But everyone knew that to get it back on track was no easy feat. It was as if we had got on the wrong bus and ended up far from our intended destination!

I therefore think it paramount that we ask two preliminary questions before even planning church-based community development activities. The first is for everyone, and the second primarily for those considering church-NGO partnerships. The first question then is: *Is the church, group of churches or diocese ready to involve itself in community development?* To answer this, we would need to ask supplementary questions such as: Does the church as a whole have the passion, heart and commitment for community development? Does the church love its surrounding community, those who are not its members? Does the church have some understanding of what community development is? Is the church willing to put its own resources into the activities for the benefit of the community? For pastors and church leaders, it is important to check whether the church members stand with the leaders' vision and heart for the community. It may be advisable to arrange meetings for the whole church or diocesan leadership team where everyone has the opportunity to say what they really think and to shape the vision, and leaders know they are not on their own. Of course, if the leadership or potential partner concludes that the church is not ready, this does not mean the end of the road. It simply means that the church should take time to prepare itself. No one wants to go to a wedding where the bride has not made herself ready. All the guests would be disappointed. In the same way, a church beginning community development before it is ready will disappoint its community, hurting both itself and them.

Second, if a church or diocese wishes to partner with an organization with expertise or skills in community development or integral mission, then both parties should ask the following question: *What is the nature and purpose of the partnership?* Secondary questions to ask include the following: How will we work together? Who has what responsibility? What do we want to achieve? What is our shared purpose? How long will the partnership continue for? And if it is not open-ended, how will we know when it is time to exit? It is also vital to ask: Are we compatible? And if so, how? To this end, the church/diocese and the organization should look at each other's values and vision. For the partner organization, it is good to ask: Is the aim to work *with* the church, *on behalf of* the church or *through* the church? It is important to be clear on this from the outset. If the purpose is to see the church *empowered* so that the church is equipped to continue the work on its own after the partnership has formally finished, then the partner organization should focus its efforts from the start towards that end, whereby the church is lifted up and enabled stage by stage. It will not do for the partner organization to take charge and then expect the church to take over later. It will likely be valuable for the church and partner organization to write an MOU together before launching the partnership, so that everyone is clear on why and how to proceed. I have found it helpful many times, when differences or misunderstandings have arisen, for both parties to read again what was agreed together, and then return more enthusiastically to our own responsibilities. MOUs are working documents and can be updated and revised if and when the need arises.

All this is to say that, whether we are a church pastor or a partner organization, we should ensure the necessary groundwork is done – and not skimp because of time – so that the church is properly ready to embark on and engage in community development.

Assisting the Church to Develop a Theological Vision for Integral Mission

"What you have done very well in the work of integral mission is to show how everything fits with the Bible," the bishop kindly informed me in one of our regular meetings. He had invited us to Mwanza, Tanzania, to assist in developing the church district's capability in holistic mission, particularly in rural ministry. He went on to describe how another church, a Pentecostal church, had gone about seeking to help people physically. "Seeing the struggles of the rural population [80% of Tanzanians are subsistence farmers], the church wanted to help them agriculturally. They bought tractors and equipment and set about helping people in food production, thrilled at the opportunity to make a difference. After some time, the members of that church began to cry out, 'We have left the spiritual mission behind!' And the project soon died." What we can see is that this church did not have a theological vision for this ministry, even though they were well intentioned, and had not shown its members how this ministry fitted into the mission of the church.

I wish I had known the importance of ensuring that the same theological agenda is shared when I first began working in integral mission and community development in Africa. It would have saved a lot of heartache. It is so easy to jump from the preliminaries (described above) to the actual work of planning projects on the ground. We can think we are on the same page and so off we go! It is unlikely that anything could be further from the truth. I do believe this is where so many, including many well-known mission agencies, slip up and the potential impact is lost. As said in previous chapters, we all live out of a story. We have a narrative that frames us. Although we may imagine and assume that the church, its leaders and its members, imbibe God's story of mission, it is more likely that what they imbibe is a mixture of the Bible, personal, cultural and political beliefs, and ecclesial tradition. To be honest, this is the situation we all find ourselves in, and it is important both to acknowledge this truth and to allow the biblical story increasingly to shape our being, thinking and doing. As we do this and share this with our churches, we all will be fitted together to join with God in his mission. To help the church develop an all-essential biblical-theological vision for integral mission, I offer the following suggestions:

Teach a Theological Vision of Mission

Sound and living theology undergirds a sound and living practice of mission. Therefore, take every opportunity one-on-one, in small groups, in the fields, on the roads, in church committees, in seminars and in conferences to share the most awe-inspiring vision, from Genesis to Revelation, of God's mission, as outlined in chapters 2–3. Pastors or church planters, burning with this mission, can teach it to their church over several weeks. They can set up discussion groups and Bible studies so that members engage personally and corporately with God's mission. Pastors, using the material from chapter 4, can ask their congregation how this vision connects with or challenges their own beliefs. Christian development workers or missionaries, when invited to preach, can speak passionately on God's marvellous plan to restore this world, a plan effected in Jesus and now carried forward by the church through the power of the Spirit. And if development workers are assisting in the church's community health education project, as they preach they can connect the project with God's larger purposes of bringing his *life* to humanity. There may be opportunities, as I had, to teach missiology to trainee pastors in Bible colleges and church and transformation courses to church planters, giving them a bigger vision of mission and church planting. When we do these kinds of things, living the story and sharing the story, before long we will see people and churches alive with the story and ready to be involved. While seminars and conferences on integral mission have their place, we should not think a single conference will do the trick. Rather, we and our churches all need a steady diet of God's mission, feeding on it regularly and seeing it from different angles, so that it seeps into and frames our life and mission.

Reveal the Place of the Church in God's Holistic Mission

As a development of casting a theological vision for the church, it is good to show the amazing place of the people of God in his mission. Sometimes it is easy to forget the privileged role we the church have. We get into the routine of church services and lose sight of our calling. We should teach members and pastors on the "sentness of the church," that we are sent by God in his mission to make all things new and we have our role to play as we lay down our lives for him and others. Sadly, Christians in Africa, who have been influenced by the prosperity gospel, often lose sight of the fact that they are to be servants of and willing to suffer for God's mission.[7] Let churches appreciate that the church is a community for the mission of God. To this end, it is wise to remind the church of its heritage in participating in God's mission. For example, René Padilla has written succinctly on "Integral Mission and Its Historical Development,"[8] which could be used to help churches see beyond cultural fads of their day to the way God has guided the church in mission.

Articulate a Whole-Life Mission Connected to a Whole-Life Discipleship

Many Christians think of mission as just something we do when we evangelize, but as we have seen mission is so much more. Mission includes the inner life of the church, demonstrating to people that God is transforming us. Mission involves family life, showing reordered relationships under the Lord Jesus Christ. Mission extends to work, revealing to people that God cares even for work and desires to see businesses that transform lives. Neighbours may be amazed at the yield on our farms when we align our lives with God. Mission encompasses the church, revealing both the compassion of God (by doing projects to alleviate suffering and poverty in the community) and the

---

7. My family and I, when once participating in a large conference in Nairobi, were told by Kenyan Christians that they could never give up what we had given up to embrace mission among the poor.

8. Padilla, "Integral Mission," 42–58.

justice of God (by calling out corruption and oppression). Mission consists of declaring in life, word and deed that Jesus Christ is Lord and inviting people to come to him. As churches see God's whole-life mission, how it involves the interplay of worship, prayer, children's ministry, men and women's ministry, the environment, discipleship and evangelism, they will dismantle the mission department, for they will know that mission involves everything. And a whole-life mission needs a whole-life discipleship to underpin it. This discipleship or following Jesus is learning in the context of real life and mission.

Show the Connection between (Integral) Mission and Community Development

One of the fundamental challenges for the church is to show how the mission of the church and community development fit together. None of the churches I worked with quite grasped the connection. There was a somewhat clunky and awkward relationship between the two. It is easy for churches to think that community development is their service to the community but still separate from the mission of reaching people for Christ. They may understand that the service can open the door for their mission, but still in their minds the two are distinct. However, if we work through the previous subsections, especially those of developing a theological vision and a whole-life mission, much of the groundwork will have been done. The belief of this book is that integral mission involves church-based community development but is in fact much larger. Or put differently, community development is one way that the church can express God's love and mission to their community. As that community receives God's wisdom and aligns itself with the lordship of Christ, its blessing and transformation advance. I will develop this in the next chapter, but as we work with the church or diocese we should lead them to consider for themselves how mission, evangelism and service connect and overlap.

Facilitate a Contextualized Theological Involvement

A further challenge a church may face is how to move from vision to practice. A church may be inspired to do something for its community but struggle to know how to utilize its biblical and theological reflections for a profound engagement with the community. Sometimes churches simply adopt programmes such as church community mobilization programmes. While these programmes undoubtedly have a place, unfortunately they often lead to pragmatic and superficial projects where the spiritual dimension is distinctly watered down. This may be because of the way in which the community is involved in the decision-making, reducing the outworking of a clear Christian approach. Although we often hear the saying "You don't need to reinvent the wheel," actually in order to arrive at a solution appropriate for the particular community – what we might call a contextual approach – we at least need to dismantle and reassemble the wheel for each place, having changed some of the components. There is no substitute for the church doing the sincere theological reflection and cultural and community mapping and then working out prayerfully how to bring them together. The aim is a theological shaping of practice whereby the local church operates out of a deeper and cohesive theological vision. I will delve into this later in more detail at the project level in chapter 7, but at this stage it is important to have introduced the concept at a strategic level.

Strategic Plans

The church may be enthused by its vision and fired up by the Holy Spirit to bring blessing to its community, but sadly progress in community development activities can all too easily grind to a halt once obstacles are encountered along the way. Issues may be connected to the activities themselves, but they may also be related to broader matters in the church or diocese. One possible aid can be the producing of a strategic plan. We have to face the fact that community development is not the only ministry of the church, nor should it be. Rather, the church will have other important ministries that will compete for the available time and resources. So it is important to think realistically about what kind of community development the church might do and how it will proceed, before embarking on it. I reluctantly came to the conclusion that strategic plans, wisely employed, can be very helpful in this regard.[9] Here I am not talking about planning the project itself – that will come later – but rather having an overall plan for the church and how integral mission and community development fit into the total life of the church.

There are many ways to develop a strategic plan,[10] and the church can take and adapt what it feels necessary for its purposes at the appropriate level. But strategic plans usually seek to answer three basic questions:

---

9. What I mean is employing strategic plans as servants (not as masters) in an inspiring but not rigid way, while recognizing that our work among communities is always more complex than first thought and so there must be room for adaptation as the situation arises.

10. There are many good resources on the internet to help with strategic plans.

1. Where are we?

2. Where do we want to get to?

3. And how are we going to get from where we are to where we want to get to?

To answer these questions, there is a whole series of issues to consider. If churches do produce a strategic plan, it will probably be best to involve a significant cross-section of the church, rather than it simply being undertaken by the pastor or leadership. The church can also take input from others, such as missionaries and development workers. The issues to work through include first the vision and mission of the church as well as its values. Having spent time in the biblical story and in theological reflection, and having got to know the community, these issues should not be too difficult to consider. These issues facilitate the church's answering the second of the three questions above. The next issues to consider are the strengths, weaknesses, opportunities and threats (SWOT) of the church, and it would be good to relate these to integral mission. It is important for the church to be honest about these issues and not embarrassed. A truthful assessment will yield much fruit in the long run. These four issues help the church understand its current standing, answering the first basic question above. The last set of issues to consider relates to the factors necessary to succeed in the vision and mission as the values are employed, strategies for achieving these factors, and some organizing activities to set things in motion. This set of issues therefore answers the third basic question above with reference to all the previous issues debated and agreed upon.

Once the plan is agreed, it is good to have regular meetings to review progress, consider ways to overcome problems and challenges, set targets for the next phase and assign responsibilities. A strategic plan should be a working document that is updated and amended as time goes by. It is vital that churches produce plans that work for them and not against them. Such plans should not be restrictive and slavish, but rather focusing and enabling. They should also spark lots of creativity.

There are at least two great benefits to the church's producing a strategic plan. The first is ownership. The plan is the church's, arising from its own passions and desires, taking account of its own resources, and it is to be enacted by the church. The second is that it helps to embed integral mission and community development within the overall life and mission of the church. Whether or not a church opts for writing an official strategic plan, this embedding of integral mission is the foundation that must be laid to avoid community development being a clumsily bolted-on activity which can fall off at any point.

Working with the Church

As well as assessing whether the church is ready for community development, and helping it develop its theological vision for integral mission and produce its strategic plan, when it comes to the daily work there are a whole host of matters which can make or break our efforts. Here I highlight a few important principles.

Building Relationships

Although I have already mentioned that everything in Africa happens through relationship, I cannot say this too much. I address this first from the perspective of the pastor and then from the perspective of the Christian development worker/missionary, although these two roles could be done by the same person. I have visited many places where the pastors or church planters have had plenty of good ideas and desires for what could be done in the community but evidently have not taken their churches with them, and in fact convey the sense of their own isolation. But if the pastor has close relationships with the members, they will naturally be open to the pastor's input and leadership, and the church becomes motivated to embrace the missional initiative. A well-connected pastor can make things happen! I remember being impressed by one village pastor on his first week in the job introducing himself to the village chairman and executive officer. But I was shocked to find that in an adjacent village the village executive officer did not know who the pastor was of the church we were about to begin partnering with. The first church became ready for meaningful community engagement whereas the second struggled on on its own.

The importance of relationship is no less important for the development workers or missionaries that churches sometimes utilize because of the skills they bring. These people may have been employed by the churches from another part of the country. But often they can have a "work" or "project" mentality with little else in their line of sight. Technical expertise is no substitute for actually becoming part of the church and sharing in its life. The church will see the person as one of them and be ready to participate in the project or missional activity. And as the person "enters" the local culture, the response to the project will be positive. I was once informed by an "expert" that because our trainers were not from the local Sukuma tribe, the community would not embrace the church's project. However, that did not prove to be the case. Our trainers embraced the local church and community, got to know the pastor well, worshipped with the church on Sundays, built relationships with community members, and acted out of humility and love for the community, such that the church and community embraced them. And even the youth and gender of some of our trainers were no obstacle. People were desperate to join the church's project.

Going at the Church's Pace

Although the pastor or development worker may be in a rush to get results, the right pace is the church's pace. Two Swahili proverbs come to mind: "Slowly is the right speed" (*Pole pole ndio mwendo*) and "Hurry hurry has no blessing" (*Haraka haraka haina baraka*). We usually experience growth in our lives step by step, incrementally. If the church is to own the community development ministry, then patience is called for as the church discusses, decides and organizes itself. It can be frustrating to the pastor who may think it better to get on with the task, but the church could well be left behind. On the other hand, there is nothing like seeing the joy on people's faces when they have discovered against their expectations that they can do it themselves. For the development worker, the wait can be agonizing as failure seems to be fast approaching, but real success comes when the church and local community drive it themselves. This principle of pace will be particularly important if the church has received financial assistance for the work. The church should be careful not to agree to the unrealistic timescales of donors.

Acknowledging Our Mutual Brokenness

On one occasion when training church planters on leading a church that impacts its community, I asked the students about the weaknesses in how the church conducted itself towards the outside community. Having discussed this in groups, one group replied, "The language we use to label them. We use harsh words when we describe them and it puts people off." As the discussion ensued, we realized that we, the church, conveyed our sense of superiority by talking down to the community. In so doing, the bridge to reach the community was torn down. Of course, wherever we look in the world we see the failures of the church all too easily, such as in corruption or the abuse of power. And so a foundational principle for integral mission is for the church, pastor and development worker to acknowledge with others their mutual brokenness. All of us are part of the broken world that God is reintegrating. As we humble ourselves before others, it is worth remembering that humility is always a winner! And by this means God is elevated in the eyes of others. When the church chooses to involve itself in this way in community development it offers the world a different view – one of genuine love and compassion. And the community will more readily receive and share in the work.

Working with the Church Leadership

When it comes to working with the church to enable its integral mission, it should be obvious that we need to connect regularly with the church leadership. Everything I have said about relationship-building is valid here. However, in reality it is easy to become cut loose from the leadership. I remember one of our bishops failing to mention the community development work in his annual report. Although the archbishop, realizing I was in the room, reminded the bishop to include such work in future, it dawned on me that I had not worked as closely with the bishop as I should have done. A pastor may be wrapped up in his or her fascinating girls' menstrual health project and not share the idea and progress with fellow pastors or the bishop so that the project might also begin in other areas. For the missionary, he or she may work with a subset of church members or employees and if not careful fail to bring attention to it to the wider church. This may be especially true if working across a diocese or church district. One of the good things in Africa is that introductions and greetings are particularly important and long ones are most appreciated! These are great opportunities to share about integral mission, particular examples, opportunities and stories of transformation.

Sharing the Vision

Sadly, politics bedevils church leadership and the African church is not immune. Decisions are made, not in the best interests of God's kingdom or the church's mission, but usually to satisfy someone's personal appetite or interest. The results can be devastating for the church and the way it is seen in the world. The antidote to a church being rife with politics is for it to pulsate with God's big vision. God works through leaders who are men and women after his own heart (1 Sam 13:14). The section above, "Assisting the church to develop a theological vision for integral mission," is one constantly to come back to with the leadership. Remind the leadership of the bigger picture and the context for the particular activities. One piece of good advice I received is to explain to the leadership how the specific community development projects contribute to and strengthen their overall vision of the church.

Embracing the Vision with Servanthood, Resources and Finances

Once the vision is seen, the next step is for the vision to be embraced and responded to. When God's story becomes the leaders' story, they will adopt *servant leadership*, a leadership that is about implementing God's plan for the good of others. Leadership never exists for itself but always to lead others by example and skill into the purposes of God. Therefore, church leaders must embrace servant leadership if the church is to offer the people and communities a different and transformative story. An attempt at integral mission through community development which does not look at the type of leadership required is unlikely to succeed. At the same time, a common failing of much church-based community development, especially in relation to experiencing sustainability, is to expect all the resources and finances to come from outside. I will explore this in more detail later, but it is important to mention this now in connection with working with the church leadership. Churches need to get their resources and budgets lined up with the vision they espouse. You find resources and money for what is important to you. The amount is not important, but it reveals the heart. The God who looks on the heart can multiply abundantly what is offered. This is not to say the church should not seek outside expertise and resources when necessary – it should – but that it should not seek those without offering its own first.

Connecting with the Church Leadership at All Levels

When we talk of church leadership, there is a raft of echelons. Churches have local churches, sections or deaneries with several churches as well as dioceses or districts, all with their own leadership. It is beneficial to connect with all the echelons or levels of leadership so that the yeast is worked through the dough. Sometimes a section of churches may be able to advise and coordinate resources to enable the integral mission activity in one of the churches to be more effective. When connecting with church leadership, committee meetings may have their place, but showing them the project in operation can capture their imagination. One evangelist told me that people could not understand the concept initially but, having seen it demonstrated, "they like it and want it!" Though a pastor may be working in one church, by inviting fellow pastors to see the work, often one or two will replicate the project in their own churches and communities. If we discuss with bishops and diocesan committees a particular church's missional project, they may be able to see a strategical expansion of the mission both there and elsewhere.

Being Accountable

When working with church leadership, it is important to model accountability and to help the church put accountability systems in place. Being accountable involves being transparent with the activities, results, successes and failures as well as money. If the church develops robust accountability systems, this will help it when it looks for help in funding from outside bodies.

Facilitating the Church's Leadership

Latent within the foregoing paragraphs is a point that needs mentioning explicitly. For facilitators, development workers and missionaries with the church, it is important to make room for *the church to lead*. The work is the church's, after all! And the church has much to offer in terms of leading the project, through its connections with the culture and government officials. For example, the church leadership may be able to offer advocacy and challenge public policy, without which the missional project may fail.

In summary, working with the church and its leadership in this way is foundational work that should bring lasting fruit. In the next chapter I will offer an approach for how to put this work of integral mission all together.

6

Integration and Integrity in Mission

Integrated Beekeeping and Non-integrated Water!

Pastor Wilfred Nduguta asked our team to assist his church in Ngudu in the Kwimba District of the Mwanza Region to set up a community beekeeping project. Beekeeping in Tanzania is a sector known for its unrealized potential. In November 2014 the then prime minister, Mizengo Peter Kayanza Pinda, a keen beekeeper himself, addressed the opportunity for beekeeping at the First Apimondia Symposium on African Bees and Beekeeping in Arusha, Tanzania. Beekeeping, far from being just about annoying bees, offers huge benefits to people and communities in terms of building sustainable livelihoods through honey and beeswax sales, the medicinal benefits of honey, increased crop yields through better pollination, and environmental conservation. Indeed, in our training in Ngudu we used the catchy saying, "No trees, no bees; no bees, no honey; no honey, no money," which poignantly highlights the link between environmental destruction and rural poverty and the opportunity beekeeping offers to reverse the process.

Having conducted some pretraining with the church on God's mission and the church, and then the initial beekeeping training, we waited as Wilfred and the new beekeepers from inside and outside the church hung their beehives in location. A few weeks later, Wilfred discovered that all nine hives placed in a forested reserve were already colonized. What is more, other beekeepers using the reserve were stunned and exclaimed, "How come your hives are already filled with bees when ours, which have been there much longer, remain empty?" Wilfred, simply stating what he and his group had done, replied, "Well, we bait the hives with wax to entice the bees to enter. To cut off all pathways for ants and other pests we ensure the area around the hive is clear. The wires used to hang the hives are well greased. And we pray to God to bring the bees!" Unlike in Western countries, where people buy packets of bees for their hives, in the majority of African countries beekeepers just wait for swarms of bees to enter their hives. But there is no guarantee the scout bees will select your hive as the colony's new home. Waiting can therefore be extremely long and frustrating! What was impressive about Wilfred's answer was how natural and unassuming it was, how it was complete, and how he gave weight and validity to each component. Before long, the new group of beekeepers were rejoicing as they sampled their delicious early and unexpected first harvest of honey.

If that was a good example of an integrated approach, here is one that leaves a little more to be desired. I was with a colleague visiting a water supply project. This was a smartly designed, cost-effective and well-executed project to bring a remote village some much-needed water. As we walked around, the quality of the workmanship at each part of the system and the engagement of the community were evident. It was obvious that soon the villagers would be enjoying pure refreshing water and, if they looked after the system, for many years ahead. After a long day we arrived back at the local base with the technicians, ready to leave. "Oh wait," it was announced, "we are going to do a Bible study first." The tired workers sat in a circle, each holding their booklet produced by a well-known mission organization, and I was asked to assist in leading the study. In addition to its being rather tacked on to a particularly physical day, the study itself was less than helpful. The passage for the day was John 2:1–11, when Jesus turned the water into wine! After working through a number of the questions posed, we came to an explanatory note. The author, realizing that Jesus's lavish winemaking might be a concern to many African Christians who because of widespread societal alcohol abuse advocate that Christians should not touch alcohol, sought to reassure the readers that Jesus's intentions were noble. We read, "In biblical times wine and beer were sometimes taken because water was often unsafe to drink and soda had not yet been invented." It is hard to imagine a worse piece of exegesis! The Bible shows many people, including Jesus himself, drinking water from a well or other sources, and even when the water was undrinkable God being capable of making it fit again to drink (Exod 15:22–27). While there is a wide-open door for the church to lead those who suffer from alcohol abuse out of bondage into glorious liberty, bad interpretation is not the way and usually does more harm than good. In our case, we missed seeing the central point – the unveiling of the bounteous nature of God in the arrival of Jesus – and utilizing it to fuel an integral mission through the project.

In this chapter, I seek to show how to think about integrating the various parts of the church's missional endeavours, which should all have intrinsic value, into a cohesive and powerful whole showing the gospel of the kingdom.

A Puzzle? What's the Right Way to Fit the Pieces Together?

Our illustration above shows that integral mission or integrated community development is far from straightforward. All sorts of questions can start buzzing around our heads. Which has prominence – evangelism or social action? Which one should precede? How do we fit the two together? Should social action be used to open the door to evangelism? Or should we keep them apart so as to convey pure motives?

I think all of us who have tried integral mission would agree that it is often like trying to finish a complicated puzzle. You have to try placing your piece in several locations before you find the right one where it fits. And for integral mission this is exactly what we need to do. Our first attempts will probably feel awkward both to us and to others. But integral mission is an iterative process, it takes time and we never completely achieve it. More than that, God in his grace still reveals his goodness and life to others even through the church's imperfect mission attempts.

Unlike doing a puzzle – and here is where the puzzle analogy breaks down – with integral mission there is probably no single way to do it. Different practitioners will decide on their own approach and many of their contrasting efforts will yield fruitful results. Furthermore, different contexts require different strategies. As we saw, even Jesus in his integral mission adopted different approaches at different times. Going in all guns blazing into a country or community "closed" to the gospel announcing that Jesus is Lord is unlikely to achieve anything except an early ticket out! Participating in mission requires receiving the wisdom of God and the leading of the Holy Spirit. After all, mission is God's mission and God involves us in his mission. Learning to rely on him and being flexible and adaptable is all part of the process. And as we do so, we will see God shape our efforts, bringing the components together, and giving some surprising results.

Nevertheless, while this book is not about providing a formula but fostering a deeper biblical-theological and culturally appropriate approach to our thinking and doing in mission, I do believe there are some helpful guidelines to developing integral mission.

God's Plan Is to Unite All Things

As we saw in chapter 3, God's cosmic plan is to bring all things together in Christ (Eph 1:10). And in case we missed the scope of the "all things," Paul adds, "things in heaven and on earth." This is a new arrangement for the uniting of the whole universe in Christ, whereby everything in creation is brought together to work properly under the lordship of Jesus Christ. Could God have a bigger plan?

In a corresponding passage, Colossians 1:15–20, which we noted in chapter 4, we read that "in [the Son] all things were created: things in heaven and on earth, visible and invisible, whether thrones or powers or rulers or authorities," and that "God was pleased to have all his fullness dwell in [the Son], and through him to reconcile to himself all things, whether things on earth or things in heaven." This shows that God's intended redemption in Christ is as big as creation. We know that sin has broken the unity God set up in creation – the relationship people have with him, the self-understanding they have, their relationships with one another, their relationship with the rest of creation and indeed all the interconnected systems in the world. And as reconciler of all these things, Jesus restores them back into working relationship with one another. The mission of the church, then, is to implement what Jesus achieved on the cross so that it becomes an experienced reality. As Sherron George says, "The fullness of our triune God and the total mission work of God fill the church and the universe, which results in fullness of life for all. Plenitude of spiritual, material, social, and emotional life comes through God's multidimensional mission action that includes evangelism, compassion, and social justice."[1] And quoting Orlando Costas, she highlights the integrated nature of this mission, saying,

> The true test of mission is not whether we proclaim, make disciples or engage in social, economic and political liberation, but whether we are capable of integrating all three in a comprehensive, dynamic *and consistent* witness. We need to pray that the Lord will . . . liberate us *for* wholeness and integrity in mission.[2]

What we can see immediately is that some of the questions of the previous section, such as whether we should start with evangelism or social action, are somewhat wrongheaded. They suggest that these two are separate activities.

---

1. Sherron George, "God's Holistic Mission: Fullness of Parts, Participants, and Places," *Missiology: An International Review* 41, no. 3 (2013): 287.

2. George, "God's Holistic Mission," 290.

Rather, good community development projects will be evangelistic in some way as they declare the glory of God, and equally, good evangelism will display God's concern for people. Since God's mission is a uniting mission, bringing together into a cohesive whole what has been fractured, so should be our involvement with him in this mission. Therefore, we should ask: How can we undertake the various components of mission, not as individual elements, but in a united way whereby they increasingly relate to and reinforce one another?

The good news is that this approach coheres well with what we saw in chapter 4 and the interconnectedness of life in Africa. Africans rightly recognize that the spirit world impinges on the physical world. So doing missional tasks separately, even if we later hope to connect them, is not the African way, nor is it likely to be the most fruitful way. And equally it is not simply a case of bringing the spiritual and physical dimensions together, say of a beekeeping project, although that is important. Rather, the ultimate aim is to bring all things together into a peaceful relationship. So, for example, beekeeping connects with tree-planting, agriculture, business, discipleship, evangelism . . . and each one is enhanced and made more effective by the presence of the others. People should also experience marriage, family and work as mutually enhancing.

Again, as George points out,

> [The availability of] the diversity of gifts in the body of Christ and the complexity of situations . . . lead us to engage in evangelism, compassionate service, and social justice at different places and times. These aspects of holistic mission are not mutually exclusive. Each must honor and be accompanied by the others. They should walk hand in hand, complementing and reinforcing each other.[3]

It is important to have this picture of unity in our minds as we, the church, carry out our mission. But is not the size of the task before us just overwhelming? Well, integral mission is a process, and starting small and working to join even just two aspects of broken human existence into a repaired state has huge significance and shines as a light of the larger mission that God will yet do in his time. It also serves as an encouragement for the church to continue participating with God in his mission while knowing it will not be completed until Jesus returns to earth.

---

3. George, 291.

The Importance of Each Part Having Integrity

Our church once received a team of visitors for a week's training in evangelism. We were each paired with a team member and sent out on house-to-house visiting. To help us strike up conversations, we departed armed with a simple questionnaire prepared by the team leader and his organization. So as we reached people's homes we introduced ourselves by saying we were conducting a survey in the area on people's beliefs about Christianity. We proceeded to ask our five questions, which included what they thought about Christianity and who they considered Jesus to be, and the fifth one, "Would you like to become a Christian?" The team leader later stated that he was interested only in this last question. And here lay the problem: the approach lacked authenticity, and the other questions were asked only as a guise to open the door for the last one. It was not surprising that this mission was not very fruitful.

In integral mission each part has integrity, it has meaning and purpose, and without it the whole is less. Take away one leg of a three-legged stool and it no longer supports you! In a project, community members can spot if we are phoney or not genuine and we may likely hear a retort like, "You are only using this project to spread your religion!" Or to satisfy ourselves as Christians we may add a spiritual component that is not well connected and appears to most not to be necessary. But with Jesus, there was a reason for everything he did, and each aspect contributed to the whole. "His mission included proclamation of the good news (evangelism), compassion, and justice. In order to embrace the fullness of God's holistic mission, we must honor each distinct part of it."[4]

In the beekeeping story at the beginning of the chapter, Wilfred did not say, "Preparing the hive is not important; you just need to pray!" Nor did he suggest that baiting the hive alone would do the trick. In my experience, many colonies of bees have left hives because beekeepers have failed to be diligent in caring for their hives and allowed pests to enter. And equally, well-baited hives have remained empty for months!

For us, as we plan, conduct or review our mission it is helpful to ask: What is the purpose or relevance of this part to the mission? What contribution does it make? What would happen if it were removed?[5] How do the other parts shape it and give it its power? How could we strengthen and improve this aspect of the mission?

---

4. George, 287.

5. E.g. an agriculture project that does not seek to attend to a land-rights issue may not result in a family enjoying their harvest.

Two further points are worth reflecting on in this section. First, even though each part of the mission needs to have integrity, do all parts have equal significance? On the one hand we could say,

> Salvation addresses the whole person and seeks fullness in all areas of life: spiritual, physical, psychological, material, social, economic, ecological, and political. We cannot ignore the personal, social, or cosmic dimensions or the historical context of mission. By our common baptism all Christians are called to witness and all forms of witness are equal indispensable parts of the whole. All are partial and incomplete. There is no priority.[6]

Or we could say that certain parts are more valuable (e.g. people believing in the Lord Jesus), so long as we do not inadvertently undercut the value of the other parts. For example, someone may come to wholeness in Christ through seeing God's order worked out in a community health education project. Readers may well come to different conclusions on this point.

This brings me to my second point: What happens if people pick and choose which parts to take rather than receiving the whole? This is exactly what Jesus faced in his mission. For instance, some people were only interested in filling their stomachs with bread rather than enjoying the bread of life (John 6). And of the ten lepers healed, only one came back to Jesus to offer him thanks and in return received a whole salvation. Our mission is to spread the goodness of God, and if certain people only want some of the goodness it is better to let them take it. It may well be that later, as we see in the gospels, they may come back for more, especially if we have presented the goodness in an interconnected way.

How the Different Aspects of Our Calling Work Together for Effective Mission

We have discussed the importance of seeing the unity of God's mission rather than just seeing isolated components of mission. And we have discussed the importance of ensuring that each part or component has its own integrity or reason for being. This leads on to the crucial question of how to bring the different aspects of the mission and our calling together into a cohesive whole.

In short, the answer, I believe, is *in allowing the biblical story of God's mission freedom to live in and through the church.* This story is an organizing

---

6. George, "God's Holistic Mission," 291.

and integrating principle for the whole of the church's life and mission. I invite you to read chapters 2 and 3 again and to reflect on the depth, breadth and indeed transforming power of this amazing story. To help us see how this missional story can be allowed by the church to be untethered, I wish to make use of the contribution of Ross Hastings in his marvellous book *Missional God, Missional Church.*[7] Although written for Christians in the West, the book's material is easily contextualizable for Christians in Africa. In chapter 6, "Mission of Incarnation and Resurrection," Hastings explores two questions. First, "given that the resurrection of Jesus reasserts Jesus's incarnate state and reaffirms the goodness of the created order, how do we become missional in a way that is fully creational?"[8] Second,

> how does the church engage missionally in a way that is properly incarnational *and* properly "resurrection-al"? Jesus, who was incarnate, has died and is now risen as the beginning of the new creation, as the Last Adam representing a new humanity. If that is true, then how does the church's mission move beyond being creational to be new creational?[9]

Hastings begins his exploration by covering much of the material we have considered in chapters 2 and 3 before showing how the three great tasks given to us, *the Creation Mandate* (Gen 1:26–28), *the Great Commandment* (Matt 22:34–40) and *the Great Commission* (Matt 28:18–20), work together as a team. He says,

> The mission of the Christian church is to be undergirded by the [aim] of God for humanity, that is, what he intended when he created humans in the image of God and more particularly when he sent the last Adam to be its fulfilment and archetype.[10]

> Christian mission operates with awareness of the nature of the human being as made in the image of God as recapitulated in Christ.[11]

> Christian mission operates within the context of the cultural mandate of Genesis 1–2, and not in isolation from it. . . . It is

---

7. Ross Hastings, *Missional God, Missional Church: Hope for Re-evangelising the West* (Downers Grove: IVP Academic, 2012).

8. Hastings, *Missional God*, 148.

9. Hastings, 148.

10. Hastings, 149.

11. Hastings, 150.

critical for the church to see evangelism within the wider context of the shalom experience and expression of the people of God, that is, within the creational/cultural mandate of Genesis 1–2 and the relationality of the Great Commandment.[12]

Mission that focuses purely on evangelism is truncated and misses the trajectory of divine intention for humanity.[13]

Helpfully, Hastings schematizes these three tasks in the diagram shown in figure 1.

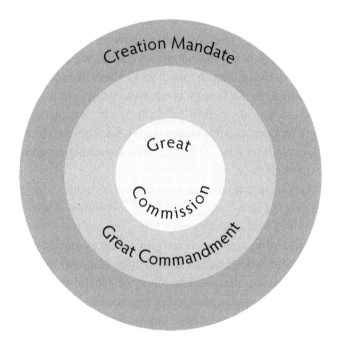

Figure 1: Carrying out mission in an integrated way[14]

Many churches in Africa undertake these tasks separately; some, especially Pentecostal churches, do not even attempt the outer circle. Some, to be fair, are working in a combined way in the inner two circles, but in my experience it would be rare to find a church utilizing all three circles effectively.

---

12. Hastings, 155. The term "cultural mandate" can be used interchangeably with "creation mandate."

13. Hastings, 156.

14. Adapted from Hastings, 156.

What is evident is that we have one mission, and that mission should be underpinned by God's purposes for humanity in creation and for the new humanity in Christ. Let us help the churches appreciate how the Great Commission interfaces with the Great Commandment and the Creation Mandate. Figure 1 shows that this can work in two ways: from the outside in or from the inside out.

Outside in: When people see Christians fulfilling the outer circle (the Creation Mandate: living out and enjoying God's original intention in marriage, family, work, farming and flourishing of creation) and expressing love for God and for neighbour, with particular concern for the poor and marginalized neighbour (second circle), this can be crucial for their journey to becoming Christians (inner circle). The church can also set up a project whereby others are drawn into experiencing the outer two circles, which may well prompt them to open the door for church members to share their faith (inner circle).

Inside out: Through the Great Commission (inner circle) people become Christians and are transformed to fulfil the Great Commandment (middle circle) and the Creation Mandate (outer circle). The church tells the full gospel (inner circle), explaining what a holistic salvation and changed life looks like (middle and outer circles).

What this shows is that whether your church is doing a single community development project or a range of projects, a blended single effective and powerful mission is within your grasp. Carrying out the Creation Mandate and Great Commandment properly are powerfully evangelistic, and it is only new people in Christ who can fulfil the Creation Mandate effectively.

In planning a project there will be plenty of questions to answer in terms of how to bring the components together organically, but this discussion has helped to frame some of the most basic questions. These include the following:

How do you ensure that a community development project is part of integral mission? It is possible to run a nicely assembled integrated community project, even incorporating spiritual and physical aspects, that yet does not provoke any deeper questions on life and lead to a whole-life and communal transformation. But good reflection should lead to a project having integrity and missional intention. It would involve thinking through how this project communicates the story of God's love and truth and invites people into it, and how the Christian participants can be equipped to share and explain it.

What is the relationship between mission and ethics? Traditionally, there has not been much consideration of this relationship, but we have seen here that this relationship needs to be working smoothly. The world sees what the church is up to and interacts with it in everyday activities. The question is, how can this engagement with the church be positive for those outside so that they see the church as wholesome and transparent?

What is the relationship between the inner and outer life of the church? This is related to the previous question. Often the church is keen to portray a good side in public, but how important is its inner life to mission? If the above discussion has shown that integrity is vital to integral mission, how can the church work towards having integrity between its inner and outer life, and what should this look like?

How and where is effective discipleship achieved? Traditionally, discipleship has been seen to begin with the Great Commission (Matt 28:18–20 and par.) when someone becomes a Christian, but is there a case for it beginning earlier? Since the Creation Mandate and Great Commandment set the context for the Great Commission, do they not also set the context for real-life discipleship? What does "teaching them to obey *everything* I have commanded you" mean? Would, for example, a transforming business project be a suitable context for discipleship? The Great Commission seems to *echo* the Creation Mandate and be a means of its renewal. For example, authority is given, and the command is to fill the earth with life.[15]

What about traditional forms of evangelism? A well-used evangelistic method in Africa has been the large outdoor meeting, but many churches are reporting that this is becoming less effective. In and of itself it does seem a lazy and fruitless approach, akin to going to the field expecting to harvest crops when you have not prepared the ground and planted the seed. But if a church labours hard in its community, carrying out the Creation Mandate and fulfilling the Great Commandment, is there not a place for such outdoor meetings as one among other evangelistic approaches? In fact, if the church does some significant groundwork in demonstrating its heart, commitment and sincerity for the local community's holistic growth, then the church may also be bold in its evangelism, utilizing a range of interconnected approaches.

---

15. In Genesis 1 humanity is made in the image of God and commissioned to procreate, and in Matthew 28 the disciples are those made in the likeness of Jesus and commissioned to make more such likenesses.

An Illustration of Integral Mission

The following is a simplified example of how working in the three concentric circles shown in figure 1 could be fleshed out in practice in a conservation agriculture project.[16]

Conservation agriculture is an ideal project for many villages in Africa as it connects to daily life for the majority of residents who often struggle to produce enough food to feed their families since the land is losing its fertility and rains are becoming increasingly erratic. Thus, the local church wanting to involve itself in God's mission has an opportunity to demonstrate the love of God in a concrete way by meeting basic needs.

First, it is advisable for the church to receive some training on the mission of God and how that mission frames and interfaces with agriculture. If the church has competence in conservation agriculture, then it could deliver the training itself; otherwise it should seek some expertise to conduct the training within a Christian framework. Second, when it comes to the training in conservation agriculture, the church could begin with a group of, say, thirty farmers – fifteen from outside the church and fifteen from within the church – all of whom are keen to learn, need the training and are willing to support one another. In the training participants can learn that God made them to rule over the earth so that it becomes abundant, and that farming is one way they can fulfil this. Being made in God's image they follow God who was the first farmer. In this way they can think of farming as a high calling. They can appreciate that their task is to cultivate the ground and to take care of the soil (Gen 2:15) – unlike in traditional farming which leaves the soil exposed to the hot sun, burning up the remaining compost in it. So combining this knowledge with conservation agriculture principles such as early preparation, covering the soil with mulch or using green manure / cover crops[17] to care for the soil so that its fertility is replenished, and crop rotation, they can put this training into action. They will hopefully see their yields at least double in the first year and continue to see further improvement in the following years.

Whereas women frequently shoulder most of the responsibility in farming, husbands can learn that in God's design husbands and wives are to work together and support one another. As the responsibility is shared, this could

---

16. This is based on real project designs and trainings which weave together theology, best practice and church-based mission, and typical results that occur.

17. These crops are legumes whose foliage grows quickly to cover and protect the soil from the hot sun, preserving the soil's moisture and smothering weeds as living mulch. At the same they fix nitrogen from the air into the soil, improving the soil structure and nutrient content. They can be dug into the soil while still young and green to further increase the soil's fertility.

bless the marriage and home, as the wife feels more valued and supported. And families may be able to expand the area they farm and grow different varieties of crops and more nutritious vegetables, with even some to sell. Fuelled with hope for farming, participants can learn to mitigate the challenges of the fall, such as through making natural pesticides to deal with pests without harming the environment. Biblical examples can inspire them that it is still possible to farm well. Cain was a successful farmer, Isaac got a great harvest in a time of famine, and the promised land was called "a land overflowing with milk and honey." They can be encouraged to heed the Old Testament prophets' call that by returning to God, restoration will follow, instead of continuing to go to the witchdoctor or pray to their ancestors to bless their land. This is a role the Christian farmers can offer, teaching God's sufficiency with no need to fear other powers.

It is valuable if the church can cultivate a quality conservation agriculture demonstration plot adjacent to the church building. Many villagers may be initially sceptical of conservation agriculture, so seeing the principles demonstrated can help them overcome their doubts. This also powerfully shows the church's relevance to people's everyday lives. Who would have thought you could come to church to learn farming! Once people are interested, the pastor and church members can then assist them to put conservation agriculture into practice on their family plots, visiting frequently to check on progress and be ready to advise on other things too.

The church can draw the community together and coordinate an effort to support the vulnerable. Widows may be helped in cultivating their crops. The poorest farmers with unprotected fields are often susceptible to losing crops through pastoralists who carelessly allow their livestock to stray. Should this happen, the church can be ready as a peacemaker, overseeing a restorative approach with both parties. Equally, pre-emptive efforts of teaching on building living fences around farms are a significant way of taking care of "the garden" (Gen 2:15).

Once a reasonable number of farmers have learned the basics of conservation agriculture and seen the benefits, the church can offer leadership to stimulate further growth and development, such as helping to set up a cooperative for farmers in the village. The church could invite a Christian business person to teach the cooperative how to run a farming business together, how to grow high-value crops or flowers, and how to gain access to markets in town. The church can facilitate training on money management, how to save, how to use a proportion of the profits to develop the business, and possibly how to offer a loan scheme. Group members will be able to use income to educate their children, start other projects or build homes, as they are encouraged to explore the ideas they have.

As the cooperative and the families enjoy the blessing of living out the Creation Mandate, the community at large may begin to see the transformation taking shape. And with the church leading the way, fostering an inclusive and sharing approach, others can be welcomed in too, with the shalom of God spreading outwards. Community celebrations after the harvest are an important feature of ensuring that God receives the praise for what is taking place.

Although there will be ups and downs, advances and setbacks along the way, the Christians and the church can in this way be a light and a blessing to the village and people may likely be inquisitive to find out more. If the church is patient and transparent when things do not quite work out, it may find that it is not hard to evangelize its neighbours. There will be an open door to share the good news of God in the grand story of the Bible. Christians can take time to explain how Jesus has fulfilled God's purpose, he has broken the chains that bind them, and he alone rules as King. They can describe how it is possible to enjoy the life God intends by believing in Jesus and becoming God's children, special and privileged. This can be in a natural setting, such as when farming together and learning about God's design. As people become Christians, church members can lovingly disciple them in how to live as God intended humans to live and as part of a renewed, joyful and just community, even as they wait for God's best. But at the same time, the pastor can lift people's eyes to see that, through aligning their lives with God in Christ, it is possible to know how better to care for creation, and to taste the abundance to come.

Conclusion

In this chapter we have discussed the need for integration and integrity in mission, and we have considered some of the important questions so that integral mission can be achieved in practice. It should be apparent that this kind of mission offers the African church the opportunity to play a bigger role in society and be a vehicle whereby God brings lasting and widespread transformation.

Rural conservation agriculture is only one example, and even here more integral mission is needed to reintegrate the other broken parts of the community into a healed and functioning whole. Integral mission can be used in urban centres as well as in rural communities. It can be employed in business, not simply to add faith to business so that selfish company owners increase their profits, but for the church to be a transforming presence in business. Then business itself becomes a means of just and equitable wealth creation leading to the renewal of communities and to playing its part in reversing climate change. Integral mission is desperately needed in the deprived and disintegrated urban areas where residents wonder where God is. And it has much to offer in education, whereby the church can lead the way once again in training children and young people with an integrated, imaginative and empowering education with the knowledge that our God reigns in all of life.

The opportunities are in many ways limitless for the church as it comprehends God's integral mission and the ways it can work with him in bringing about his integration and wholeness. As is often said, "Think big, start small!" And with that we are ready to begin planning the particular expression of integral mission the church feels called to embark on.

7

Designing the Project to Enable the Local Church to Participate More in God's Mission

A Desire to Help Our Community but Little Forethought

There are many ways a church can effectively participate in God's mission to benefit its community, but this is not one of them! Many years ago, our church, of which I was pastor at the time, was increasingly getting God's heart for mission, particularly with reaching out practically. We contacted the local town council who suggested we help with the "clean-up" week. Having agreed, we were then assigned a particular neighbourhood to clean up. This neighbourhood was known to have various needs and social challenges, with some of the residents also known to the police.

I think several of us in the church felt particularly good that we were displaying our love for these people, who in our view especially needed it. On the clean-up day we saw a lot of rubbish in the streets, which we gathered into bags. There were old items of furniture, worn-out mattresses, car parts and even broken electrical appliances dumped for all to see. Our team also recovered a motorbike abandoned and hidden in an overgrown ditch. As we concluded our work, the place looked clean and tidy. Surely the residents would be so pleased with us that they now had a nice place to live in!

Actually, even before the end of the day, I was beginning to feel that we had missed the mark. We had not engaged with any of the residents, not even with a single conversation! The only comment we received were the words, "I don't know why you're bothering. All the rubbish will be back there next week!" It dawned on me that we were doing what *we* wanted, not what *they* wanted. We were seeking to impose our values on them. All we achieved was to convey to this community that we considered them untidy and less than us. And if we had stopped to think even for a minute, we would have realized that the rubbish was not the problem, but just a symptom of a deeper issue. We made no attempt to build relationships, to understand the community, to hear their priorities and pleas, and to discuss how we might work together. Our day, I concluded, did more harm than good!

Two Basic Principles to Keep in Mind

The purpose of this chapter is to help the church and its community development practitioners, having taken on board the material of the preceding chapters, to think through the steps of how a project can be appropriately designed as part of the church's involvement in God's mission. There are, I believe, two important basic principles to keep in mind throughout the process:

- Engage the community well in the planning.
- Ensure a strong framework of integral mission.

As long as these principles are embedded in the process, the precise outworking of the design phase can vary from place to place depending on the nature of the church and of the community. Churches can think through the right approach for them and adapt what is suggested below as they see fit. It is the *manner* of the church's engagement with its community in this phase (e.g. expressing love, honour, appreciation of its neighbours) which is important, so that the church by its approach conveys God's love and heart for people. And it is the *framework* of integral mission, into which the project ultimately agreed upon is placed, which is vital, so that the church joins with God in what he is doing in the community. With these principles in place, we embark on describing the process of designing a project.

Start with Listening

When it comes to taking steps to thinking about working as the church in our community, the place to begin, I believe, is with listening. It is common in East Africa to see a group of men sitting on stools or benches outside a house in deep conversation on any topic from politics to business, sport, women or solving someone's particular problem. As you watch, you see everyone giving his definitive opinion without waiting for the current speaker to finish, and usually one chap, maybe someone smaller and younger, desperate to get his view across and failing, before shouting exasperatedly, "*Sikiliza! Sikiliza!*"

("Listen! Listen!"), in a last attempt to be heard. So many societies in various cultures and countries struggle with listening, not just in the present day but down through history. The apostle James, writing in such a context, says, "Everyone should be quick to listen, slow to speak and slow to become angry" (Jas 1:19). Of course, we are often slow to listen, quick to speak and quick to get angry, which does not produce the desired results, nor as the next verse goes on to state, "the righteousness that God desires."

Listening is a wonderful skill. When we listen, we value the opinion of the other above our own. When we listen, we build relationship. When we listen, we humanize. When we listen, we learn. We are ready to discover more. We are open to new possibilities that we had not seen before. When we listen, we hear the faint sounds that our noisy world drowns out. Though they may be faint, they may also be the most important sounds. Sometimes, the wisest words, or cleverest ideas, come in the faintest voices of the small child, hardworking mother or old man who will not force their views on others but offer them only when asked.

One of the best things about listening is that when we listen, we are humble. Another is that when we listen, we are wise. Proverbs 1:5 says, "Let the wise listen and add to their learning." Two prerequisites for taking good steps towards community development are humility and wisdom, which come through listening and result in learning. So at the outset, the church should adopt *the posture of a humble listener*. By this, I mean two things. First, the whole church, including the pastor, the bishop, the missionary, the development worker and the newly graduated theology student full of ideas, should listen. Very often the more education we have, the more we struggle to listen and the more we miss. Second, when I say "be a listener," this does not mean we should not speak or dialogue or ask how what the person is saying is true – of course we should do all these things. But we should not assume we know what is best but rather seek to dignify others. What I mean is that we should be quick to listen and slow to speak. There will be plenty of time for giving our views, but in the first instance we should be seeking to learn with genuine, heartfelt and compassionate listening.

When we as a church give priority to listening and learning, taking in many perspectives, we are more likely to have a community development initiative which is well thought out and appropriate to the local community. We could call it a *contextualized response*. It is easy to rush to copy and paste ill-thought-out ideas that have not been honed for our location. Missiologist Dean Flemming defines "contextualization" as "to do with how the gospel revealed in Scripture authentically comes to life in each new cultural, social, religious and historical setting."[1] And remember that the gospel, as we saw in our journey through Scripture, is a full-blown gospel of the kingdom that touches everything! In order to contextualize well, to see God's great story live well in our community, to know what the particular response is that God calls us to offer to and with our community, it is helpful for us to do *four listenings*. These are:

- Listening to the Bible
- Listening to and being aware of ourselves as a church
- Listening to the community outside the church
- Listening to the Holy Spirit

It is important to realize that these four listenings are interrelated and not what we simply do separately or sequentially. Let us however outline each listening in turn.

Listening to the Bible

It is vital to understand God's mission and our mission from the Bible: who we are and our role in the world, who Jesus is and how he carries out his mission, what the church is and how it is to carry out its calling, and what God's end purpose is for us and creation. All this we outlined in chapters 2 and 3, but it was only an outline. By listening to the Bible, we hear God's word to us. We reflect on it deeply, contemplate it, and allow it to encourage, confront and form us as God's people. As we appreciate not just individual or isolated verses but the whole sweeping story of God, of how the parts fit together into a cohesive whole, we will be increasingly shaped by the biblical story so that it becomes our story as we live it. In this way, our worldview will be healed and transformed so we see the world biblically and know our place in it, as we saw in chapter 4. I encourage us to let the framework of the story of God's mission revealed in Scripture be the framework of our mission. We should make sure the big ideas/themes of the biblical mission are the big ideas/themes of our mission.

This listening to the Bible is not a one-off event at the beginning, but an ongoing process – conducted daily, weekly, monthly, yearly! We can be ready to ask questions such as the following: What is God saying to us? How does the Scripture inspire us? What are the aspects of mission we have not seen

---

1. Dean Flemming, *Contextualization in the New Testament: Patterns for Theology and Mission* (Leicester: Apollos, 2005), 14.

before? How does the biblical approach challenge our cultural assumptions and worldview? How do we need to repent?

We can do this study, reflection and dialogue in all kinds of settings – small groups and large gatherings. But I would encourage as many members as possible – young and old, male and female, educated and uneducated, leaders and ordinary members – to be involved in this process. In this way, it will be immensely forming for the whole church community.

Listening to and Being Aware of Ourselves as a Church

This listening is in some ways a continuation of the previous one, but now focused on the church community and its relation to mission. This is an opportunity to listen to and dialogue with one another. We can ask questions such as: What is our history and story as a church? What is the make-up of the church? What does the church have vision and motivation for in mission? What are the church's gifts and strengths that could be utilized in mission (e.g. prayer, land, lots of entrepreneurs)? What are the church's weaknesses which need to be addressed so that it can be effective in God's mission (e.g. syncretism, laziness, lack of love)? How can the strengths be harnessed and the weaknesses be overcome so the church can respond passionately and positively to the community's situation? What training does the church need in order to be more effective in integral mission? Answering these questions is an opportunity for the church to consider its story, identity, vision, gifts and passions and at the same time to be honest about its weaknesses, gaps and challenges so that it is suited and ready for the particular missional project that will commence.

Listening to the Community outside the Church

The church should not think that the first two listenings are sufficient but should humble itself and engage with the local community. Obviously, the church and its members are part of the local community and may share some of the same views, but at the same time listening to the community will give the church a different perspective too. This is what Paul does in Acts 17:16–34 in Athens before he preaches. He walked around the city, effectively surveying it, he reasoned in the synagogue and the marketplace, and he debated in the Areopagus, learning the local issues and philosophies. This all helped him to craft a suitably powerful sermon later.

It is important for the church to ask leading questions to understand the community's stories, worldview, symbols and practices. What are the community's values (these could be good and/or bad)? What are the community's successes and how did they occur? What are the opportunities and issues? What are the community's struggles? What are the community's hopes? What are the sins (e.g. corruption, witchcraft, abuse of the poor)? What are the cultural idols (e.g. power, money)? Which religions are followed (e.g. Islam, animism)? What is the social reality of the community? It will be valuable to explore with people the reasons for their answers to many of these questions. Invite people to diagnose, to consider the causes (people and systems), and to suggest potential courses of action to capitalize on strengths and remedy weaknesses to bring change. All these findings will affect how the mission is conducted.

In doing this, it is vital that the church engages with a wide cross-section of the community. If one talks only to leaders, the men and the more prominent people, the view the church gets will be skewed, although these perspectives should not be avoided. So think through how the whole community can be represented in some way and the voices of those often ignored, missed or sidelined (e.g. women, children, the poor, the weak, the less able) most certainly be included. Remember, these will be among those who need the project the most! It will be good to engage with the community in a variety of formats – house-to-house visits, small groups, larger gatherings. The church here is seeking to understand people's perspectives and so good active listening is required, asking follow-up questions, inviting people to explain their reasons, offer their suggestions and reflect on the community's circumstances. To this end, a carefully put-together survey can be useful, so long as those producing the survey have a clear sense of what the survey should achieve. But we should recognize that a survey is only a tool and a servant and that interviewees should be allowed to go off the survey in their sharing since valuable information might be revealed. It is also wise to test the survey on a few people first to check it achieves the intended job. If not, it can be revised before being used with many people. After gaining all the perspectives, we should seek to map the community, collating the history, the story, key events and their outcomes, the opportunities, key challenges different groups face, assets in the community, values, hopes, and so on.

Listening to the Holy Spirit

We know that without God's enabling and direction we will not succeed. And it is *his* mission, not ours, so listening to the Holy Spirit is essential. He may have highlighted things in our listening to the Bible, to ourselves and to the community, but we should also bring all that we have heard and place it at his feet and allow him to speak. Waiting in the Spirit's presence is a great skill for the church to learn. God confounds the wisdom of the wise, the community development experts, and reveals his wisdom to the humble. He may give us insight into both the causes of the situation and the remedies. This is also an opportunity for us to lay down our desires and agendas to gain God's desire and agenda for the community.

Synthesize These Four Listenings

These four listenings, if done well, will take time. They cannot be rushed. Once they have been done sufficiently the next task is to synthesize them, to bring them together into a whole. The beauty of this process of the four listenings is that we should end up with something which is *biblically inspired and framed*, *church-based*, *community-relevant* and *Spirit-led*. To do this, the next sections can help us.

Needs-Based versus Asset-Based Community Development

There has been a debate in recent years over whether one should adopt a traditional needs-based approach or an asset-based approach to community development, with people increasingly jumping on the asset-based-approach bandwagon. It is helpful first to briefly outline these two approaches.

With a needs-based approach, the aim is to discover the problems or needs, what is not working or not there, so as to fix the problems or supply the needs. This approach has fallen from favour for several reasons. First, it emphasizes what is wrong with the community. Second, the needs have traditionally been diagnosed by outside professionals who may not have sufficiently involved the locals. These two lead to the third reason, which is that the community feels bad or deficient. Fourth, the solutions have often been proposed by the outsiders and result in the necessary resources being supplied from outside. And fifth, this results in the community being minimally involved and not empowered.

In contrast, the fashionable asset-based approach focuses not on a community's needs but on their resources or assets. It looks at what they possess – their assets, skills and talents – and seeks to mobilize the community to use these things to improve the life of the community. In this way, the community is involved in its own development and can make use of what is increasingly known as a "circular economy."[2] Christians involved in asset-based approaches point out that this recognizes the blessing of God already present (e.g. strength, time, land, animals, entrepreneurial skills, community togetherness) and the gifts bestowed. Even Jesus, before the miracle of the feeding of the five thousand, asked his disciples, "What do you have?" After searching, they presented to Jesus the five loaves and two fish in a despising way. And as we know, when offered to him, Jesus can use the little we have and work wonders!

So which is the better approach? Although at first sight the asset-based approach looks more promising – and has achieved some good results – I think we should not be too quick to dispense with the needs-based approach. True, the way I presented it needs modifying. It can be used by the community itself and does not have to rely on outside experts from Nairobi, Kampala, Dar es Salaam or Kigali. The solutions and resources do not necessarily have to come from outside the community. We have to face the fact that every community, wherever it is in the world, has problems or needs that must be addressed if sound community development is to ensue. And sometimes we need outside assistance to help us see clearly, and there is no shame in that. The world could not simply mobilize its resources to make itself a better place; it needed Jesus to come into the world to deal with the problem of sin. As this book is about integration, it probably comes as no surprise that I advocate *an integral approach*, taking the best from both approaches as we consider the whole picture – indeed, we will have to integrate other issues too, such as rights-based issues. It should seem obvious that this approach is the best course of action. An asset-based approach which fails to look at the very real problems in the community is unlikely to achieve much lasting benefit, nor is a needs-based approach which does not make use of what the community has but relies on external assets. A reflection on the whole picture to harness the strengths and what is working well in the community to address the weaknesses and what is not working in the community provides a healthy structure. As Nordstokke says, "Before diagnosing what is *not* there in a person, family, local community, or society that should be – a 'needs-based' approach – an asset-based approach

---

2. In contrast to a linear economy in which one starts with raw materials and makes a product, which is thrown away (take-make-dispose), a circular economy reuses, remakes and recycles materials and products, aiming to maximize value and eliminate waste. Its value to Africa is being explored by the African Circular Economy Network (https://www.acen.africa/).

asserts that it is important to understand what *is* there of crucial significance for the health of the public."[3]

In my experience, when communities discuss matters, with the aid of useful questions they naturally pick up needs and deficiencies themselves and someone or a few will propose ideas or offer resources to address those needs and suggest the community pulling together to achieve some goals and aspirations. The Swahili word *harambee*, widely used in community fundraising, means "pulling together," and it is in this spirit that people need to approach community development. There are all kinds of approaches and methods variously nuanced, but what is required is *good facilitation* so that the church or community can consider the situation appropriately, whether or not it knows about the methods.[4]

Preparation Is Key

Even after good listening, there is still much more preparation to do, before we begin. Sometimes we are so keen to get started, as we have been inspired by the *what* and the *why*, that we fail to discuss the *how* and the *who*. Even our *what* may need further refining so we move from what we could do sometime to what we should do now in terms of community development. To ensure good preparation there are a number of points to be aware of:

The Process Can Be As Important As, If Not More Important Than, the End Result

In terms of the church being empowered for integral mission and connecting well with its community, the process by which preparation is made is essential. We have already encouraged a good beginning to the process in the suggestion of starting with listening. Listening engages people and draws them together. If the end goal is community development, then the community must be drawn together, be actively involved and learn to work constructively in the planning process. Even if the end decision is not as extensive as, say, the pastor had hoped for, if a good process has been used the community will be ready to implement

---

3. Nordstokke, "Faith-Based Organisations," 199.

4. In my opinion, Westerners are often fixated on method and model, believing that the right one will guarantee good results. This often results in failure as previous wisdom is cast aside uncritically.

the project and foundations will have been laid to attempt something greater in the future.

Participatory Approaches Start the Project before It Starts!

When the poor, the marginalized and those normally overlooked get involved in the planning phase, their empowerment has already begun. Ensure there is good dialogue with all stakeholders by asking probing questions, exploring their responses and seeing what solutions they can propose. As their ideas are incorporated, even if modified, you will see increased buy-in and ownership. To be part of the solution is incredibly energizing. In my opinion, good leadership is required to ensure there is adequate coordination of the participation so that discussions are framed well and move towards healthy outcomes.

Collate and Analyse What Has Been Learned through the Listenings

By this point a lot of data will have been gathered through the listenings. It is time for a balanced and representative team to begin to make sense of it all. The team should look for common themes, connections and causes (appreciating spiritual, physical, intellectual, cultural and communal interrelated causes), and prayerfully and reflectively propose appropriate actions to bring transformation. It is advisable to check these with church and community members to gain widespread agreement and to receive adjustment. In this way, the team should arrive at good project ideas.

Begin Sifting All the Good Ideas to Settle on the Ones for Now

Next comes the task of narrowing down the possibilities for now. This, we should be reminded, involves prayerful reflection and waiting on the Holy Spirit. One helpful tool in this is to make use of the vision triangle proposed by my former colleague Andrew Wingfield, shown in figure 2.

This vision triangle can help us know where to begin. Although we may wish to begin at the top with the biggest ideas, as with building a house we should begin with the foundation. Using our own resources first will likely lead to a more sustainable effort and enable us to be ready to know how to appropriate outside help properly in the future. We should ask: What are the foundational building blocks? What are the secondary building blocks that rely on the first ones? We should also ask questions such as: What do we have faith for? What do we have energy for? The aim is to arrive at something the church with the community can realistically undertake by also depending on God.

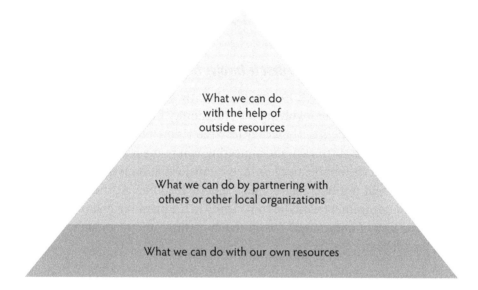

Figure 2: Vision triangle for being active in transforming our community[5]

Check Your Skills and Resources and Consider Any Necessary Training and Partnership

In helping to decide how best to commence our community activities, there are further areas to think about, which include the following: What skills and resources do we have? What skills and resources do we lack? How can we best mobilize our competencies as a community? Can we put together the right team to oversee matters? What training do we still need? Is there expertise either locally or regionally that we could call upon? Will we partner with anyone? If so, for what purpose and extent, with whom, and would we be compatible (see chapter 5)? Just because we may not have all the skills and resources for the particular project idea does not necessarily mean it is the wrong project. At the same time, if we have hardly any of the necessary skills and resources we may need to think again. Before moving on, in my experience communities sometimes need encouragement to think "outside the box" when it comes to

5. Adapted from a training presentation by Andrew Wingfield.

resources so as to think beyond money! It is not uncommon for the initial response to the question of what resources they have to be "nothing," only to discover after probing they have quite a few. And we should remember that, as we saw in chapter 4, biblical and African approaches to poverty alleviation include a communal sharing of resources for the common good.

The Church Should Decide How Best to Involve the Community in the Process

A key issue for the church to consider is how best to involve the wider community. A danger in involving the community in an unreflective way is in the church surrendering a biblically inspired vision for renewal. Sometimes all the church does is to convene a meeting where the community decides what to do and the opportunity for deep transformation is lost.[6] The wider community will not likely have God's agenda in mind. At the same time, insufficient engagement with the community in the planning phase will likely result in a lack of interest and commitment by the community later. This all calls for wisdom!

Designing the Project

The design phase of the project is really an extension of the planning phase. Some readers will choose to do some of the issues about to be mentioned earlier as part of the initial planning. To my mind, there is no right order, and different situations call for different approaches. Once there has been good listening and sufficient engagement with church and community members in initial planning and a settling on the issue(s) to tackle and at least some of the causes, it is time for active work on specifically designing the project. At this stage the purpose is to shape a project which enables the church to participate more in God's mission, leading to the blessing and building of the local community. In this, we seek to follow God the designer (Gen 1). The following are the crucial elements in the design phase.

---

6. This could be called the "lowest common denominator" approach. In my experience, though this method is commonplace in Christian circles, it is unable to sustain a biblical-theological-missional framework from conception to design to implementation, which lies at the heart of this book. Very often it seems to end up in mere pragmatics!

Who Designs the Project?

The first element is to get the right designers. We have consistently mentioned the importance of ensuring an extensive participation in the planning. But when it comes to the design, clearly it is not feasible or advisable for the whole community to be directly involved.[7] If the aim is an integral mission project, then logically it should be the church who gently and humbly leads the shaping of the project. In practice this will be a capable group or team, variously skilled, and mainly but likely not exclusively from the church, which works on the design, making use of what was learned through listening and participatory initial planning. This team will wisely continue to consult with those outside, testing the design to gain feedback from the community and taking expert advice where necessary. Against the grain of current opinion, I believe it can be beneficial sometimes to include on the team outside help in a field where wisdom is lacking (e.g. integral mission, technical skills). Also the team should have good representation of the project's participants. So if it is a project for youth, then youth must be part of the design team. If it is for women's empowerment, then different women have to be involved in the design. And if it is an agriculture project, then active farmers should be shaping the project.

Develop a Framework for Biblical Transformation through the Project

The next element is to work on the architecture of the project. The focus here is on taking the project idea(s) and setting it/them in the framework of God's story of mission. If it is a community health education project, then think through what God's intentions for healthy communities were at creation, how the fall has broken those, and how God responds to bring healing through calling Israel and supremely in Jesus, and now extended holistically through the church, leading to the hope of wholeness in the new creation. How will the project declare the power of this story of healing and wholeness, integrating the personal, family, communal, spiritual and creational dimensions? In doing this, consideration will need to be given to how the biblical story interfaces with the results of the listenings to ensure a contextualized framework and engagement (e.g. how God cares for vulnerable and disenfranchised people to ensure their rights). How will the project help the participants to recover something of God's design, who they were created to be, able to form and to

---

7. If the community is the whole village, then there could be at least 1,500 to 2,000 people! So sufficient but realistic representation of the various members is important.

fill? How can the biblical story connect with and transform the people's story? How can this project foster good stewardship of creation, making sustainable use of the resources God has given?

Define the Place of the Church in the Project

While the place of the church as a people in the project should be evident if the previous element has been done well, it is important to set this down explicitly. It is vital that the project and the church are relationally and visibly connected. How will the life of the church strengthen the project? How will the church's integral mission be carried out through the project? How will people experience God's truth, knowledge, compassion and love through the church? How will Jesus be seen in the church through the project? How will the people be challenged to follow Jesus? How will the church lead sacrificially in working towards fulfilling the project (e.g. funding the project, offering resources)?

Specify the Expectations of the Project

Another essential element in designing a good project is in specifying clearly what the project is expected to achieve. Fuzzy expectations often lead to disappointment! Who are the intended participants and indirect beneficiaries? What is their age range? What is the scope of the project? What will the people become and what will they hopefully achieve through the project? What will it not achieve? A key point to bear in mind is to set attainable expectations in results and timescales so the project does not overpromise and underdeliver!

Assemble the Vital Components to Achieve the Project Idea

Many components must come into place for the vision or idea to be realized. What are these vital components? What training is needed, and how does it enable the other components? How will the resources be harnessed? How will the community be mobilized? What are the challenges in the community's worldview that need to be overcome for the project to succeed? What is the nature of poverty (see chapter 4) and what are the appropriate courses of action? What are the rights issues that should be addressed for participants to be able to enjoy the fruit of their labours? How will there be knowledge-sharing among the participants? How will the stronger ones support the weaker ones so that expectations are fulfilled? How will integral mission be specifically and practically designed into the project?

Work on a Sound Method for Implementation

With the basic framework for church-based integral mission in place together with clear expectations and knowledge of the project's vital components, we are in a position to set out a method for implementing the project. Here it is important to spell out the *who* and *how* issues noted above. Who will fulfil which responsibility and how will the tasks be done? For example, who will monitor the progress and how will the training be conducted? How will identified risks be mitigated to avoid project failure? The *when* question must also be addressed: When will the various tasks begin and finish? Remember that some tasks will not be able to commence until others are completed and so timescales should be realistic. There may be various phases or stages to the project. How is it going to be possible to move from the first to the last stage? What is important in this element is to show how the various phases, aspects and steps contribute to one another and fit together. In an integral mission project it is fundamental that all the parts hold together. Someone looking at the design should be able to tell that this is a well-designed project that hangs together and is likely to succeed.

Write a Project Proposal/Plan

All the above elements should make writing the proposal straightforward. The parts of a simple project plan are as follows:

1. Introduction: introducing the church (and its partners) and work in general, and then introducing the project.

2. Reason for the project: why this project is needed, with some research and statistics and what others are doing.

3. The methodology of the project: how it will be executed, the steps of the project.

4. The outcome of the project: how people's lives will be improved and how the need for the project will be fulfilled.

5. The budget of the project.

Sometimes, especially if outside funding is to be sought, a more detailed proposal might be needed. In this instance, a *logframe* (logical framework) may be required to set out the plan in a logical way to show how the phases and their time frames fit together. Logframes require the project's activities, anticipated outputs, outcomes and impact, together with indicators showing the achievement of the last three items. Be aware, however, that logframes have arisen from a Western context which values measurable data, and not everything can be measured. Indeed, much of what is most important to human beings – our relationships to God, ourselves, others and the rest of creation – cannot be measured easily, especially in a two-to-three-year project, although with effort some deeper and more holistic measures can be employed. Therefore, to prevent the project concentrating only on the less important and easily measured issues, it is vital to set the project first within the larger framework of the biblical story of God's mission (outlined above) to ensure the fuller architecture is considered. Otherwise, instead of building a cathedral, we might only build a shack! Communities need to be inspired with a bigger, indeed God's, vision of transformation.

The Issue of Money and Fundraising

Money is a thorny issue when it comes to community development. A church's faith in God to do all things can easily evaporate when it sees the budget! The vision triangle (figure 2) can be helpful in determining the appropriate scale of the project. I believe that whatever financial resources a church may have, it is usually beneficial for the viability of the project if the church contributes something financially. As Jesus said, "Where your treasure is, there your heart will be also" (Matt 6:21). We put our own money and resources into what we value most! If the church and community can financially resource the project on their own, there will likely be a more sustainable transformative project, even if progress is slow.

Sometimes it is necessary to seek outside funding in addition to what the community contributes. At this point extreme care is required. Some donors offer funding but take back control. As a friend of mine says, "You stop doing your project and start doing their project!" It is wise to look at the mission and values of potential donors to check they are a good fit. Christian organizations and churches are usually easier to work with as their interest is in assisting the local community. Non-Christian organizations may insist on a secular project. The church should resist the temptation to compromise to get money – it is a matter of faith. Donors generally have some guidelines for granting funding so if they are deemed suitable another proposal will need to be written to show how the project fits with their criteria.

Finally, it is paramount that all project funding is spent on the particular project and in line with the stated aims. Nothing destroys the credibility of the church faster than its misappropriation of money! With this in mind, at this stage the church should set in place a system for complete financial accountability and transparency.

An Example: An Entrepreneurship Project

An entrepreneurship project is a splendid opportunity to promote real community development in which community members generate and enter enjoyable, valuable and profitable work. Peter Greer says, "After looking at the data about what transforms poverty-stricken communities in a lasting way, we have come to the conclusion that if you care about helping the poor, you must simply care about business and entrepreneurship."[8] In terms of participation and empowerment, an entrepreneurship project ranks among the best options.

Here I will sketch some of the crucial features that a church may like to think about in designing an entrepreneurship project to facilitate its integral mission. I will do so by using the elements mentioned in the "Designing the Project" section above. I will assume that in the listening and initial preparation phases some potential business opportunities to help the local area and community have already been identified.

Who Designs the Project?

The main questions to answer here are the following: How can we put together a well-balanced team comprising business expertise and biblical-theological awareness, and also integrating skills, local knowledge (especially of markets) and intended participant representation? Second, how can the assembled team utilize the listening data to ensure a contextualized project?

Develop a Framework for Biblical Transformation through the Project

For this element, it is worth thinking through how the chapters of the biblical story relate to entrepreneurship. First, how can participants appreciate the connection between their being God's image-bearers and their work, so that they achieve productive work through stewardship of the resources God has given? How can they follow God the entrepreneur to use their creative abilities in work as they participate with him for the flourishing of all creation? What opportunities exist to renew "the wastelands" outside "the garden"? Second, because of the fall, what are common failings of business that should be

---

8. Peter Greer, *Entrepreneurship for Human Flourishing* (Washington: AEI Press, 2014), 6.

addressed? How can the temptations of selfishness and misuse of people be avoided? Third, how can business serve as a model of God's transforming purposes to employees, customers, family and the wider community? What kind of business ethics are seen in the Old Testament law and Proverbs, especially in relation to honest work and generosity to the vulnerable? Fourth, how does Jesus shape discipleship through business? How does his reply "Did you not know that I must be about my Father's business?" (Luke 2:49 NKJV) connect being a son or daughter of God to our work? How can business produce wholesome fruit? How can the Great Commandment feature in business to build a healthy business and to avoid the temptations to love money and build bigger barns? Fifth, how can the church demonstrate Jesus's vision of the kingdom in the context of daily work integrated with family and worship? Sixth, how can the vision of the New Jerusalem guide the entrepreneurs towards social justice, community-building, shalom and fruitfulness?

Without taking this element seriously, a church may end up with an entrepreneurship project which leads only to profits for business proprietors who could misuse their new-found wealth in selfish gratification, and the chance for wholesome and wider transformation would be lost.

Define the Place of the Church in the Project

How can the church show God's wisdom through creating business opportunities for work relaunched as a means of transformation? How can the church be a forum to bring the fledgling businesses together for training, mutual encouragement and support? What is the place of Bible studies and prayer? How can the church ensure that its interest is in supporting transforming lives rather than in seeking financial rewards?

Specify the Expectations of the Project

One key expectation would be the project reaching the people who need business skills the most to become self-determining business owners. Another expectation could be to decide on the number of sustainable businesses with an average number of employees operating at the end of the project. A third expectation could be the contribution of the businesses to the shalom in the community, for example by improvement in family life, the satisfaction of customers and neighbours, and the inspiration given to others.

Assemble the Vital Components to Achieve the Project Idea

Vital components of the project could include the following: business and community transformation, correct selection of participants and business ideas, seeing creative opportunities, training in Christian entrepreneurship, businesses that are different, ethics and discipleship, financial management, ability to repay loans, accessing markets and business mentoring.

Work on a Sound Method for Implementation

The method for executing the project could have the following phases:

Phase 1 – preparation: Awareness-raising on the value of Christian entrepreneurship, selection of participants by the agreed means, collection of baseline data.

Phase 2 – training: Training in entrepreneurship (e.g. business as transformation, Jesus as entrepreneur, having a big vision, choosing your business, market research, business practices, ethics, customer care), writing a viable business and financial plan (with request for a percentage loan), approval of business plans and granting of loans.

Phase 3 – businesses begin: Entrepreneur groups start businesses, training and mentoring (record-keeping, overcoming challenges, money management, marketing, developing the business, loving your customers, investing, creative thinking, depending on God, learning, decision-making), support meetings hosted by the church, promoting businesses, sales, repayment of loans and monitoring.

Phase 4 – businesses grow: Continued support meetings hosted by the church, business expansion, evaluation, and celebration of God's goodness.

8

Participating with God to Carry out the Project Faithfully

We Are Off!

"I am so excited! We are finally starting the project." It feels good to begin at last. We may be filled with hope for what the project might achieve – that people will experience life in all its fullness. Or we may have a sense that we as the church are doing what we are supposed to be doing, being among our community ministering to the needs of our day. We are following in Jesus's footsteps as he spent considerable time, not in synagogue "committee" meetings, but among the ordinary people in their towns and villages, attending to their needs. Jesus's mission was always practical, connecting with the struggles of daily life.

The wait may have been excruciating. If outside funding was sought, it could have taken several months to find out if we were successful and receive the money. (It can be sensible to apply to more than one funding body as refusals are sadly not uncommon.) Or we will have been busy in other preparations, such as communicating with local officials, continuing to build relationships with community members or arranging the right facilitators or trainers, all of which take time. In this waiting period, prayer is essential as we ask God to bring all the foundation stones of the project into place. There are many hurdles to jump and we cannot do it without him. And as God answers our prayers, through achieving funding, acquiring gifted personnel or blessing from officials, our faith is built up, as we know for sure that this is God's doing.

Since God has brought us successfully to this beginning point, let us launch the project with prayer, committing it to him, asking for his enabling and submitting ourselves to him. It is his work after all. We are not asking him to join us; we are committing ourselves to join him, the senior partner. Depending on the nature of the community, if you can engage the participants in this prayerful launch, you can open them up to the sphere of God's activities. Even if it is a strongly Muslim community, it may still be good to include appropriate prayer with the participants, since Muslims also recognize the need for God's help.

Doing What We Said We Would Do
The Project Proposal

The first thing to do is to reread the project proposal. It may be many months since you, the pastor, the development worker, the missionary or the person responsible wrote the proposal. It is important to familiarize yourself with it once again – its plans, approach and timescales. *At the basic level it is imperative to seek to do what was promised.* The proposal was carefully thought out and offers the essential framework. It will only cause us problems later if we are negligent in fulfilling the stated activities. For instance, if there are financial donors we may undermine trust and reduce the chance of obtaining future funding. It is also part of our being accountable to the participants who will have been involved in the planning phase. Of course, necessary changes can be made, so long as we have good reasons and discuss these first with the relevant people.

Well-Planned Activities

Once we have brought ourselves up to speed with the proposal it is time to turn our attention to planning the project activities well. One of the first activities to plan will be how to obtain good baseline data[1] against which we can check the progress of the project. When it comes to training and meetings, we should make sure that we have contacted the participants in good time (and more than once) and agreed all the particulars, we have all our training materials and equipment ready and we know what we are doing. This may sound obvious but many projects fall down because of poor planning. I remember one trainer calling us wondering why no one had arrived. When we asked, "Did you contact them to arrange the meeting?," they replied with embarrassment, "No!" The person had travelled three hours to give training that had not been arranged! Although many problems can occur, often outside our control, as far

---

1. E.g. for a sanitation project, such data will include the types of toilets people use if at all and the kinds of diseases present and their prevalence, as well as how people describe the state of their health.

as it concerns us as facilitators and trainers it is paramount that we are diligent in planning properly and offer something of quality.

Good Record-Keeping

Record-keeping is an essential task to master. There is nothing worse than trying to write a project report without data! "How many students were trained in tree-planting? How many trees did they plant? How much income did the school get from the tree nursery?" "Oh, I am not sure" is not an acceptable reply. What I found invaluable was carrying a logbook with me wherever I went. You can jot down details as you hear them, and note people's challenges and successes. You can write up your larger findings and what was accomplished at the end of the day. It is also good to write down people's stories when you hear them. Increasingly, these are being valued as better indicators of success beyond statistics as personal community stories shed far more light on what is being achieved. When there are meetings with participants it is essential that minutes are taken to ensure an accurate written record of what was agreed. Even though the secretary of the group should do this, you as the facilitator should ensure you get a copy. Sometimes misunderstandings arise over apparent agreements, but by turning to the minutes they can be quickly settled.

Good Financial Management

If the project uses money – although it should be understood that not everything we do in the community does use money – then the need for good financial management is a given. This includes keeping receipts for all purchases and getting the best price. It also includes keeping track of the expenditure, comparing the actual with the budget for each category. In many ways, the budget is a best guess. Sometimes we can underspend on one category and overspend on another; there may be flexibility to move money around and it may be prudent to do so. But in most cases, there is little we can do about the total and we should work within that figure. Therefore, we should regularly review the financial situation of the project and make decisions that lead to the meeting of objectives. There may be occasions when it is expedient to seek further funding to achieve outcomes if there were unforeseen factors.

Regular Meetings

Holding regular meetings to review progress is another vital feature of implementing the project well. We may hold these with project participants, church staff, local leaders and trainers. We can ask questions like, "Are we on track? What challenges are we facing? Do we need to make adjustments? Are we ready to move to the next phase? Are we employing well the model of three concentric circles for integral mission [see figure 1]?" It is important to encourage a forum in which everyone can share his or her honest perspective which is then valued. In this way, on the basis of good evidence you can move forward as one team with all participants knowing their responsibility as a contribution to the whole.

Monitoring and Evaluation

Monitoring and evaluation are two more indispensable tasks of project management. Myers defines monitoring as "the routine collection of information that shows what has been accomplished (or not accomplished) over some limited period of time."[2] And then, explaining why it is done, he adds, "The community and the holistic practitioner use the information from a monitoring exercise to make adjustments to program plans, budgets, and time lines."[3] Three points are in order. First, as suggested in the Myers quotation above, the participant community should be involved in the monitoring exercise. If they are to be empowered and own the project, they need to be responsible for what they have done, measure the progress and come up with any necessary mitigating actions. Clearly, the pastor and facilitators should also be involved, to see it for themselves and to assist the participant community to undertake this task thoroughly. Second, monitoring makes use of the logframe (see chapter 7 above), but one should ensure that one assesses the overall shape of the project (not just the obviously easily measurable things, such as the number of new mothers who participated in the breastfeeding training). Third, connected to the previous point, listening to people's stories can be truly enlightening as these combine personal, spiritual, social, economic and environmental realities. If integral mission is about inviting people into the story of God who heals their own broken stories, this is where we learn most about what is being achieved. At the same time, transformation takes time and we should be patient for these stories to come forth. They cannot be forced!

---

2. Myers, *Walking with the Poor*, 288–89.

3. Myers, 288–89.

Evaluation is usually the task that is done at the end of the project to assess what has been achieved, whether the project fulfilled its objectives, and possibly to offer some follow-on recommendations. Donors generally require evaluations, often by a qualified person outside the project. Evaluations can therefore hold a certain dread for those who oversee the project. But one piece of advice I received is that, if we do our monitoring well, we do not have to fear the evaluation. Even if an external evaluator is involved, it is also advisable that practitioners and participants do their own evaluation, since monitoring and evaluation are about "learning our way to a better future."[4]

Maintaining Relationship with Donors

Another important task, and one that is easily overlooked, is maintaining a good relationship with the donor. Sometimes donors require regular reports, but even if they do not it is advisable to make yourselves accountable to them with the regular flow of communication. It shows that we value donors and see them as an integral part of the team. They in turn feel appreciated and know that their money is showing a good return in the lives of precious people. If possible, invite the donors to visit you to see the project with their own eyes. Sometimes, problems arise with a project and the sooner you can inform the donor the better. A couple of times when we were facing significant challenges because parties were not fulfilling their responsibilities, I was open with the donor. He wrote back saying, "Thanks for letting us know. Don't be discouraged. There are always challenges in doing God's work." It was such an encouragement to the whole team. A year later that donor contacted me and said, "We have some money left over. Could you make use of it?"

The Facilitators' Approach and Commitment

What we discussed in the previous section is like a skeleton. A skeleton provides support and structure to the body and protects the organs, among other functions. But in and of itself, a skeleton is lifeless. We need to put flesh on the bones! This section and the ones that follow are about bringing the project to *life*. But we need to remember that, just as without a skeleton a human being is just a blob on the ground, so is a project without good management. We need to attend to both, just as we saw in creation when God forms and fills. Without the forming, the life would have dissipated. So let us work with God in his way.

---

4. Myers, 287.

In this section, I will look at the facilitators' approach and commitment. By "facilitators," I mean those who oversee the project and work with participants so they flourish. These could be pastors, church officials, development workers or missionaries. It is worth reflecting on the following areas showing the attitude and heart of those involved in overseeing and facilitating the project, as these can be instrumental in the project bearing good fruit.

Presence and Relationship

The facilitators' presence and relationship with the participant community is the foundation of a healthy project. Africans are relational people, and influence and successful reception of a project come through the closeness and personal connection between facilitators, trainers, church leaders and participant community. Working together in relationship is what causes what we do to be enjoyable, encouraging and meaningful. It makes a project feel multidimensional as a network of healthy relationships is opened up in which, I may add, God's own presence is also experienced. It is important that the participants feel that facilitators and trainers are with them every step of the way. I would say that presence is more important than technical know-how: that is to say, a trainer with exceptional know-how who is insufficiently present may be less successful than another with average technical skills but who is always seen, is encouraging and is with the participants.

This aspect of presence and relationship is two-way. As church officials and trainers build relationships with the community, appreciating and valuing them, getting to know them, emphasizing their equality and common humanity, the community may want to do something in response. For example, in many villages hospitality is still an important value[5] – sadly it is being lost in the cities – and you cannot expect the project to be received if you refuse their hospitality because of time. On the contrary, as you accept the kind offer of food, you both appreciate your host and have the chance, as you wait the hour or two while the food is prepared and cooked, to dialogue with those gathered about how the vision of God's designs for community, the project and their stories interface.

---

5. See Timothy J. Monger, "An East African Perspective on Jesus as Revealer of the Father through His Use of the Friend at Midnight Parable as a Means for Teaching Powerful Prayer (Luke 11:1–13)," in *Who Do You Say I Am? Christology in Africa*, Africa Society of Evangelical Theology Series 6, eds. Rodney L. Reed and David K. Ngaruiya (Carlisle: Langham Global Library, 2021), 25–42.

Christian Living

When the participant community sees the project overseers with them and living out their Christian faith, this is highly motivating and inspiring and increases participation. Church leaders and trainers exhibiting humility, love, kindness, compassion, grace, truth, commitment, faithfulness and honesty draw participants to them as they see something of Jesus in them. Sometimes, participants may have doubts as to whether a principle advocated by the project will really work, but through relationship and the Christian character of the overseers they will trust them and commit themselves to trying the principle. Out of love for the people, a facilitator may stop to pray for a troubled participant or take the person to hospital. And when mistakes are made by the facilitators, in humility they should freely admit them, and the respect in which they are held will grow. Overall, the facilitators' authentically living out their Christianity is a known factor in leading the community towards transformation.[6]

Continuous Training and Adaptive Teaching

One common mistake that is made is to think that the initial training seminar will "do the trick." I have seen both expatriates and Africans surprised and frustrated when the training did not lead to the expected fruitful results. Sometimes people do not even try to implement the material or perhaps implement it poorly. When it comes to delivering training, there are two important questions: Do they get it? And will they do it? There are of course skills we can learn to make the teaching interesting, varied and memorable, and we can ask participants to reflect back what they have learned to ensure the teaching is as effective as possible. But equally, training needs to be repeated and rolled out appropriately in a variety of settings and ways. None of us grasps a concept fully in just one session. Community forums can be good means of learning in which members who have already understood can help the others to look at something from a different angle. They can foster ideas, best practice and the respect for local knowledge as challenges arise, and enable teaching to be effective for the context.

---

6. So Myers, *Walking with the Poor*, 350.

Teamwork

Implementing projects as a team – with the project coordinators, church officers, trainers and key local participants operating in unison – can be far more successful than working in isolation. The various team members complement one another. Some will be better technically, others people-wise, others in seeing how the parts fit together and still others in record-keeping. Being part of a team can also help us overcome difficulties. I remember visiting one village with one of our agriculture trainers. Participants were against the nitrogen-fixing inedible jack beans she was suggesting be intercropped between the maize. "Why would we put poison in our fields?" one asked. So we sat down, listened to their concerns and then did an impromptu seminar from first principles, with diagrams about the benefits of these jack beans which instead of being poison were actually green manure. At the end, everybody wanted the jack beans, with one farmer saying he would plant five acres of jack beans to keep up supply for others. Our wonderful trainer had done her best; all it needed was help from a colleague who could approach it from a different angle. At the end of her time, she was honoured by the village for the amazing work she had done.

When the Unexpected Happens (And It Will): A Chance to Learn

Implementing a project is never straightforward. There are always unexpected challenges and disappointments. There may be natural disasters, differences in the expected rainfall, pastors moving, people dying, relational difficulties . . . the list is endless. We just need to be prepared for something not to work out as hoped. There are a few things we can do to chart a course through the challenges to a place of blessing.

Foster a Community Spirit

In community development it is the life of the community that ultimately matters. So whatever kind of project is being done, whether urban or rural, it is wise to encourage a community spirit. This is a traditional African quality. Communities get through difficulties together not as individuals. Ask questions like: How can we do this together? How can we support one another? How can your gifts complement another's weaknesses? How can we cooperate together? Emphasize the "we" over the "I." Even if the difficulties are relatively minor, the fruit of the project will still be greater. But if big trouble strikes, the participant *community* will be better able to deal with it.

Not a Problem, but a Challenge!

I was often encouraged by my African friends, "It's not a problem; it's a challenge!" By seeing it as a challenge, they focused their efforts on circumventing the obstacle. This relates to the previous point in that finding a fresh approach is easier when you are not alone. And in terms of building resilient communities, challenges are in fact a blessing.

Learning and Growing Together

One of the reasons why we face challenges is because we have never been this way before. Myers's phrase "learning our way to a better future" is absolutely the right approach.[7] There is no blueprint for success. A community which learns and grows through a particular difficulty can be set up for something bigger. When a problem occurs, a good first step is for the participant community to sit down together and discuss matters. If the church pastor or trainer is present, he or she may be expected to supply the solution. However, even if pastors or trainers believe they have the answer, it is better that they simply facilitate the community's own discussion and its moving towards its own proposed solutions. This is essential to the development process and yields better results in the long run. The group may need to consider if there are wider issues in play. If some members are doing well and some suffering, it could be beneficial to ask, "What are the first group doing different from the second?" This is known as "positive deviance." It tends to drive change from within the community rather than looking for external help, which could be called upon as a last resort. Most of all, this is a chance to pray and gain God's wisdom.

Good Fruit Comes Not Because of Our Plan or Abilities but Because of God's Involvement

Whether or not big problems occur, the fact is that the project does not produce good fruit because of our smart plan or clever abilities (even if we have them), but because of God's involvement. Paul, who considers himself "a wise builder," tells the Corinthians, "I planted the seed, Apollos watered it, but God has been making it grow. So neither the one who plants nor the one who waters is anything, but only God, who makes things grow" (1 Cor 3:6–7). Here we can play to one of African culture's strengths and encourage dependency on God. There is a huge role for the church here. It is vital we engage the faith of the

---

7. Myers, 287.

people, even if they are non-Christians. Both Elijah and Elisha engaged the faith of the women who came to them for help (1 Kgs 17:7–24; 2 Kgs 4:1–7). Both stories involved oil and describe the women being requested to do what was unnatural. In Elijah's case, he was outside the land of Israel and dealing with someone outside God's people. By following the prophets' instructions, the women experience a remarkable turnaround. And the widow at Zarephath exclaims at the end of the episode, "Now I know that you are a man of God and that the word of the LORD from your mouth is the truth." With regard to engaging the faith of the participant community, I wish to mention the role of the word of God and prayer.

Communal and Contextualized Bible Studies

If God is the author of transformation, then as the participant community engage with him through the Bible, they open themselves up to know him and his purpose and to experience his work in their lives. In my work, I have seen the role of Bible studies to be highly transformative. Many African cultures are much closer to biblical cultures than their Western counterparts, making connections with daily life easier to spot.[8] Context will guide as to the best approach in using the word of God in the project. Special care should be taken when participants who follow other religions are present, so as not to undermine the integrity of the project. Bible studies which are about the community exploring and discovering together in an open way through question and answer what the Bible has to say are generally particularly fruitful. In my opinion, these are to be preferred to someone simply downloading his or her thoughts. As the group learn to ask good questions of the text and read it themselves in context, their eyes will be opened to its value, not just to the project, but to the whole of life. Bible studies which relate to the particular project in some way are especially beneficial. They contextualize the reading of the Bible, demonstrate how integral the Bible is to the project initiative and reveal the Bible's wisdom to the task at hand. The Bible is full of wisdom for agriculture, animal husbandry, community health, business, gender equality, leadership, students, and so on. To this end, putting together a series of Bible studies that takes the participants on a journey through the whole of Scripture can lead to spectacular results in terms of personal and communal formation, giving them a platform for other things as well.

---

8. E.g. many African cultures are agrarian and so people appreciate the biblical links between land and livelihood.

Relevant and Centring Prayer

Another way the participants can see their communication opened up to God is in prayer. Because Africa is a spiritual continent, prayer is likely to be a rewarding avenue to explore. Help people to see more of God's involvement and concern in their daily lives and the project will be life-changing for them. Praying to God in all phases of the project should be natural for the community and an opportunity for some less prominent members to grow in prayer. Celebrating answers to prayer in achieving desired outcomes is all part of the participants' learning to see God's power. Recognizing God's pre-eminence in community development and his being the main actor will set the community on the right course. Prayer is a welcome corrective to Western approaches which emphasize the community's moving towards self-reliance and out of dependency. Instead, prayer moves the community towards reliance and dependency on God, with their actions as the outworking of their God-given responsibilities.

A particular role for the church is to uphold the participants and the project in prayer. By being intimately connected with the participants, church officials can bring news of the project to congregations and pray for needs in church services. Another useful practice is for the church to hold regular prayer days, either for the project or with the participant community.

I remember the first time I worked with a church in community development. The place had experienced extreme deforestation, with people taking twice the time they used to take to collect firewood. I was asked to begin a fuel-efficient stoves project in which a group of villagers from inside and outside the church would be trained to make portable clay stoves that they would then sell to the village. These stoves offered health, environmental, economic and gender-empowerment benefits (see chapter 10 for more of the story). Each working day we began with a Bible study and prayer. Then we moved on to making the stoves from the clay we had found locally. After some time, having made sufficient numbers of stoves and fired them in the kiln, the group began excitedly to sell the stoves. But unfortunately, before long reports started coming back that the stoves cracked on second or third use. How disappointing! We tried to improve the manufacturing process and did everything we collectively could think of, but without solving the problem. Finally, I stood up and told the group, "I don't know what else to do. This clay is not good enough. We need to turn to God in prayer!" This the group did.

A little later, two of the women were out in the forest collecting firewood and happened to chance upon a big mound of clay. They took a sample and the group tested it and found they had discovered better clay. God had answered their prayers. The solution did not come from human ingenuity, or expert wisdom, but from God alone. The group discovered for themselves that God was with them and that success rested with him.

Mission Happens through Love, Service, Struggle and Hardship

God's mission is an awesome mission to transform everything, every people, every community. And yet how in a world with challenges and which often opposes God is this mission achieved and carried out? This is a huge question for us and the church to wrestle with as we face challenges in the community, government officials opposing us or even feelings of personal inadequacy. We can be helped by having a good perspective, knowing that mission and community development happen through love, service, struggle and hardship. To these we now turn.

Love as the Cause and Motivation for Integral Mission

The Bible shows that God's mission is *because of his love*. John 3:16–17, Romans 5:6–8 and 1 John 4:9–10, for example, display what mission looks like. It involves costly love. And it is at the cross that we have *the clearest picture of who God is*. The cross displays God's magnificent love! His glory! God gives himself! No love, no cross; no cross, no mission! To a hostile world that hates him he responds with love. He overcomes rebellion, insubordination, misuse of power, not by an expected show of power to crush it, but by the opposite – love. God takes all that evil can throw at him and defeats it in the cross (Col 2:13–15; 1 Pet 2:21–25). Dean Flemming says, "Jesus' whole mission is a concrete expression of the loving character of God."[9]

In the same way, love is to be our motivation in sharing through the projects in God's mission (cf. 2 Cor 5:14–15). Jesus's death is the basis for a new covenant of life for all peoples and Jesus calls us, his followers, to deny ourselves, take up our cross and extend the blessings of this new covenant to the world. It is our love for Jesus and for others that propels us forward. Love gives the right shape to mission and our involvement in community development. Other motivations can distort our efforts and leave people damaged. Love shows the character of God to people so that they experience his goodness. It recognizes the extreme value of people as those made in God's image and aims

---

9. Flemming, *Full Mission of God*, Kindle loc. 1946.

to dignify, lift up and empower them. In the trials we may face, let us reach out to God for his love for the community.

Service Is the Practical Demonstration of Love

My colleague Peter Beatus says, "No life for others if we don't put ourselves out." Service is about pouring ourselves out for others and it reveals our love. In serving others, we follow the Lord Jesus who said, "For even the Son of Man did not come to be served, but to serve, and to give his life as a ransom for many" (Mark 10:45; cf. Phil 2:6–8). Service is the outworking of love! Our focus through the difficulties and challenges, sometimes with difficult community members or government officials, is on the good of the participants and this enables us to persevere. I remember once talking with Peter about the challenges in one of the projects and in particular about one person who was not participating. My advice to Peter was not to continue with this man as in my opinion we were wasting our time. Thankfully, Peter did not listen to me but continued his work of service with the gentleman, which for some time seemed fruitless. However, in the end, this man became not only an excellent farmer with a wonderful papaya orchard, but also one of the best trainers of others.

The Place of Vulnerability, Weakness, Struggle and Keeping Going in Mission

Why do we often face disappointment and struggle in our mission? The answer may involve a combination of the following: (1) our own mistakes, failures, personal issues and sin; (2) the participant community's mistakes, failures, personal issues and sin; (3) being in a broken world; and (4) the clash of the kingdom of God with the kingdom of darkness. And yet none of these are reasons to give up, but rather to keep going, for in our struggle, weakness and perseverance God's goodness is revealed both to us and to those we serve. When we are vulnerable, weak and struggling, it may be a sign, not that we are on the wrong track, but rather that we are on the right track. Paul says it so well in 2 Corinthians 4:7–12:

> But we have this treasure in jars of clay to show that this all-surpassing power is from God and not from us. We are hard pressed on every side, but not crushed; perplexed, but not in despair; persecuted, but not abandoned; struck down, but not destroyed. We always carry around in our body the death of Jesus, so that the life of Jesus may also be revealed in our body. For we

who are alive are always being given over to death for Jesus' sake, so that his life may also be revealed in our mortal body. So then, death is at work in us, but life is at work in you.

This passage shows that weakness is a strength in mission, since it is only through our being cracked and like easily breakable jars of clay that Jesus's light shines out and his life flows out to others. Therefore, it is best that we become at home with our weaknesses, struggles and disappointments and allow the cross to become the centre of our mission. We may not fulfil all the project aims but we can play our role in allowing the community to move towards appreciating God and his aims for them.

Celebration

Africans love celebrations! And celebrations feature prominently in the life of Israel, especially in the annual festivals which both commemorate their deliverance from slavery in Egypt and offer gratitude to God for the harvest. Celebrations at the end of the project or at significant staging posts are an appropriate opportunity to attribute all success to Almighty God who has faithfully been with the community. Just as with Israel's festivals, community events are an opportunity to rejoice in the Lord, thanking him for the transformation he has brought and for his provision. If the project has led to successful agriculture or animal husbandry, why not encourage the community to bring some of the fruits for a communal celebratory meal? And if the project has made use of some new technology, let the celebration acknowledge God who enabled the technology to be designed, installed and used for the benefit of the community. Then the technology will not be seen either as having solved the community's problems or as a new form of witchcraft. Let God be given all the glory.

A Testimony of Patient Integral Mission: It Works!

This is the story of Khadijah (not her real name) from the Mwanza region in Tanzania. Khadijah was a Muslim woman with five children and an unsupportive husband who came and went. As you can imagine, life was hard for Khadijah. It was her job to provide for her children, a job she, with little education, was ill-equipped to do properly, but nonetheless she struggled on as best she could. The lack of joy in her life always showed on her face. To make matters worse, Khadijah had a child with albinism, which brought shame from her husband and others and discrimination against her and her children. She became connected to a support group for similar women. This group met twice a week and together these women learned to make various craft products to raise their household incomes. But they also prayed and studied the Bible together, considering who God created human beings to be and their given task, and how God cared for the vulnerable and powerless, those whom others shamed such as Hagar the Egyptian slave and Rahab the prostitute. Khadijah saw the opportunity and worked hard, taking responsibility for her life and the lives of her children, and she noticed her income increase.

But Khadijah also had another problem, diabetes which she struggled to manage, although a kind Christian helped her with the cost of the medication. At one group meeting she arrived upset, worried about her infected finger which was very black. She had been to the hospital and been told that it was showing signs of gangrene and would need treatment immediately – treatment she could not afford. The other women, alarmed, prayed fervently for God to heal her finger and then sent her off to the hospital straight away with money for the injections from the group box. When she saw the doctor, he was amazed that in the time that had passed the gangrene had not spread along the finger, into her hand and arm, but had in fact travelled in the opposition direction out of that finger. The doctor said to her that he had expected not only to amputate her hand, but possibly her whole arm. God had miraculously healed Khadijah! From this point on, Khadijah frequently reminded the group to pray together, now knowing the power of prayer. None of those Christian group members were ever allowed to forget to pray! God was evidently at work in Khadijah. The group continued to meet week by week without fully knowing what God was doing in her life, until one day Khadijah announced that she had become a Christian! She joined a church and was baptized, and from then on the joy of the Lord showed on her face!

This story occurred over about a four-year period. Khadijah was first welcomed freely into a supportive group which unlike her family gave her love and acceptance. In reading the early chapters of Genesis (often a good place to start with Muslims), she could see for the first time who she was created to be, and in particular that she was created to have responsibility over at least part of creation – her life and her household. She learned the skills to become an artisan so as to fulfil that responsibility. As well as helping her in her work, the weekly group prayer and Bible study also facilitated her growing understanding of who God was to her, which he also later revealed to her by dramatically healing her. At the right time it was only natural for her to become a Christian and join a church.

The story did not end there. One day Khadijah and another group member stole a large amount of money from the group. Instead of kicking her out of the group to fend for herself, the group decided to forgive her (and the other woman) and set up a challenging but realistic arrangement for her to repay all the money in eighteen months. Khadijah experienced God's lavish grace, a fresh chance, which she, broken at the time, gratefully received, and her discipleship in Christ grew. Khadijah is now debt-free and not looking back.

9

Being Captured by God's Larger Purpose and Wider Mission

Introduction

While it is important to make every endeavour to do what we said we would do, it would be a mistake to limit our efforts to that, to have "tunnel vision," so to speak. As we saw in our journey through the Bible (chapters 2–3), God's vision of transformation is holistic and expansive. Therefore, it is part of our Christian witness to work towards this, and rigidly limiting ourselves may even harm the project we are doing. How can we move from seeing just the project to expanding our involvement or attending to other matters as well? To put it another way, how can the project serve and lead on to the wider purposes of mission and not be an end in itself?

Ezekiel's Story: Eating, Family and Wisdom

Ezekiel was one of a group of young men in a village where we were living and working with the church. He embraced life, was hardworking and at twenty-three years old was the church choirmaster. Most of the other men in the group had completed primary school, though one or two had not even been given the opportunity or support to do that. Ezekiel was the only one who had any secondary school education but, we later discovered, he had been forced to leave in the second year because of an eye problem. We could see potential in these bright young men. So every Wednesday evening we invited them to our house for a Bible study where we journeyed through the Bible to see what it had to say on the theme of leadership. It put to good use the Bibles they had been given in connection with the project. The contributions of these young men were fascinating and insightful as they reflected on the Bible and their culture and how God was calling us all to lead differently. Ezekiel stood out particularly. He was small in stature, but once we were able to help him with glasses he was eager to read the Bible, not only in these studies but at home, too.

Over the course of time, Ezekiel offered us the following perspectives. First, after we had all enjoyed rich fellowship and lovely meals together, he declared, "I thought we Africans couldn't eat with *Wazungu* [white people], but I know it is not true any more." Second, one day, after we had officially finished the project and moved on, Ezekiel needed to come to town, a three-and-a-half-hour bus ride away if the worn-out bus did not break down. So I invited him to stay the night with us. He recounted to me the conversations he had had with his fellow villagers when he told them he was going to town. "Oh, where are you staying?" they enquired. "With *ndugu* [family]," he replied. And Ezekiel added to me, "Well, it's true, isn't it?" And of course it was. Third, Ezekiel, who we knew devoured the Bible and read it with his family, shared, "I love the Bible and especially Proverbs." And then he testified, "Do you know what? I'm becoming known as a person of wisdom!"

What this story shows is that Ezekiel was coming into his new identity in Christ – as somebody with immense stature and a full and equal member of the body of Christ, the family of God. This was beyond the scope of the project proposal but very much within the scope of God's agenda. In this chapter, I consider *how we can partner with God to go beyond our initial thoughts and project focus to be open to his larger and deeper agenda.*

People Matter More Than Projects: Not Only Doing What We Said We Would Do

An important foundation for moving beyond the initial agenda is seeing whole people and whole communities before projects. Projects exist to serve people and communities, rather than people and communities existing to serve projects. An African mindset is so much better suited to this than a Western mindset, which tends to be task-oriented. Clearly, at the beginning the church will need to concentrate its efforts on launching the project successfully, but a genuine love for the community will ensure that the church has a healthy perspective in its involvement with the community. People and communities have a variety of interconnecting needs and with a heart of compassion the local church will be well placed to respond appropriately. Even as the church attends to so-called "side issues" or unrelated matters that locals raise, they may find that, by displaying their sincere heart and concern, motivation for the project is enhanced.

Lifting Our Eyes to See the Bigger Picture

As well as having a people-centred approach to community development, another prerequisite for an increasingly healthy approach is being open to see the bigger picture. Africa is a continent that loves football. You can connect with almost every young African man by talking about football – African football, English Premier League football, Spanish La Liga football . . . in fact, any football. And if you have a real football, so much the better! Children will even make "footballs" by wrapping bags together into a sphere. Such is the pervasive enjoyment of football. My daughter gave me a book by journalist Steve Bloomfield entitled *Africa United: How Football Explains Africa*[1] which shows the interface between football and the various political and cultural issues of the time. Lifting your eyes to see the bigger picture for community development is akin to keeping your eye on the ball when playing football. Strikers, by focusing exclusively on the ball, can do the almost impossible in their unbelievable dribbling, going past defenders one after another and so turning a match around. And goalkeepers unfortunately can turn a match another way by dozing off, letting a simple shot squirm through their hands into the net.

"Keeping our eye on the ball" for us is keeping our gaze fixed on what God is wanting to do in the community. The project is a part but never everything! Keeping the bigger perspective in mind is essential as we carry out the project to avoid not being able to see the forest for the trees. As we keep in step with God, maintaining our life closely with him, we will pick up his heart for the community among whom we are working. Specifically, to help us gain God's heart, we can do the following:

Prayerfully Dwell in the Biblical Narrative

As we spend time in the biblical story, God will unveil the riches of his mission, surprising and cajoling us in ways we had not imagined. As we reflect on the multitude of episodes and accounts in the books of the Old and New Testaments, we will see fresh revelations of God's character and concern for us to emulate. His story is told in so many places, settings and times and among so many peoples, some you would least expect. We will notice connections here and there, how these individual stories fit into and contribute to the larger tapestry of God's overall story. The challenge for us, after many weeks, months

---

1. Steve Bloomfield, *Africa United: How Football Explains Africa* (Edinburgh: Canongate, 2011).

and years of toiling in our work, is never to allow our appreciation of God and his purposes to grow stale. There are always familiar passages where we can glimpse something fresh as well as new vistas to see. There will be ideas and thoughts of things we can add to work towards a more rounded mission. And by detecting God's compassion for the destitute widow or the people of Nineveh, we may be prompted to ask ourselves, "Are we adequately sharing his desire to reveal his goodness to all people? Which people are currently being excluded in our work? Who is missing out on justice?" By "all people" we should be careful to remember all peoples *horizontally* and all peoples *vertically*.[2] By spending time regularly in God's presence personally, with colleagues, with church staff and members, and with the participants, we will be energized and inspired to move with God and follow him where he is going.

Keep Our Ear to the Ground

God often speaks to us through the voices of the community. These may be cries and pleas or ideas and suggestions. Can we pick them up? Do we hear them? The smart fisherman senses the faintest tug on his line and reels in the fish. Sometimes the pleas and suggestions come amid our busy agendas. We may be in the middle of some intense training and a quiet voice at the back says, "Why don't we . . . ?" God still often speaks in the "still small voice" (1 Kgs 19:12 NKJV) that is easy to run roughshod over, and not always in the booming call. What is important is that we keep a record of the requests and ideas from the community or others and present them prayerfully to the Lord.

So often these two points, of dwelling in the biblical narrative and keeping our ear to the ground, work in unison. One may lead to the other, and if we have eyes to see and ears to hear what the Spirit is saying to the churches, we may surely know how God is leading us forward. And attending faithfully to these two points is an essential way we exercise godly leadership through the project and beyond, and it paves the way for the following section.

Asking Wise Questions

The previous section sets the context for us, the church, to participate in God's larger purposes for our community in which we can ask wise questions. At one

---

2. The word "horizontally" emphasizes different people groups, especially those we would not naturally think of, such as the unpleasant people of Nineveh, while the word "vertically" highlights the various strata in society, specifically the people at the bottom like the widow.

level, many good questions will already have been asked in our monitoring and evaluation, and we should be careful to make those processes work for us. Monitoring and evaluation are painstaking exercises that involve a lot of work and warrant a greater airing than just being for the donor's report. They often contain the seeds of the next phase. So it may be sensible to consider how you are going to use the monitoring and evaluation findings. But there are also many other questions we should ask to help us discern God's will for further work, and I outline a few now.

How Can We Add Value?

We can ask this question at any stage, and asking it mid project is particularly valuable (no pun intended). There may be ideas and opportunities to add components, sometimes at relatively minimal cost, to enhance the project and bring real benefit in the lives of the participant community. To all intents and purposes, these features are originally unplanned but very worthwhile and demonstrate a flexibility with the community as opportunities arise. Our efforts to produce a sound project proposal are at best half-sighted and we should be looking to make adjustments and add components along the way. For example, colleagues overseeing a community health education project with four churches on Kome Island in Lake Victoria, where new mothers were being taught the benefits of exclusive breastfeeding, added a VICOBA[3] component after a few months. VICOBA is a community microfinance scheme in which community group members buy shares each week and operate a monthly loan system to one another. Community members therefore have access to loans to begin entrepreneurial activities to get themselves out of poverty. This successful scheme facilitates the community acting together to benefit one another. In the case of the new mothers' group, beautifully supported by the local pastor who was a woman, each week when they came together for breastfeeding training they also "played" VICOBA. This gave members added incentive to participate in the health training, which resulted in a greater number of healthy infants as well as boosting household income.

We may also think of ideas that are not strictly in line with the project. Teaching a group of people to read, for example, can add tremendous value to their lives, not least in their ability to read the Bible for themselves and to be able to access other training opportunities. Urban churches near universities with student ministries can run leadership programmes for the students, many

---

3. VICOBA stands for Village Community Bank.

of whom will go on to places of influence in the nation. As well as teaching the students what godly leadership in the spheres of life looks like, churches might also like to think about adding value with students encouraged and supported to exercise leadership by beginning new ministries to benefit the local community.

Where Can Greater Strength Be Built into the Community?

Computers have hardware and software and both are needed and required to work together if the operator is to avoid extreme frustration and not be tempted to throw the computer out of the window. But the same is also true of projects. They too have hardware and software components. For instance, in a water project the hardware consists of the pipes, tanks and tap stations, all of which the community may assist with in digging, building and installing to a high standard to ensure a functioning system. But without good software the system may never be utilized to its potential or may fall into disrepair early. Software is the inner dimension of the project, including how the project is perceived by the community, whether they own it or not, how they will manage the system so all have access to the water, the knowledge of why and how clean water is vital to life, the understanding that water is a gift from God as a resource for the community to manage well, and so on. In many ways, the software side is more important than the hardware side. And the hardware may actually be easier to install than the software. Frequently, community developers have not paid enough attention to this software side and have seen disappointing results in the community.

This software side is in fact where true empowerment often takes place in the mind, heart and life of the community. And it is usually much cheaper. In my experience we can always enhance the software side and there are scores of opportunities for the local church to set the agenda in this even beyond the scope of the project. The beauty of investing in the software side of community development is that it can set up the community for exploring other opportunities on its own. At this stage, the project may have set a good foundation for the church to involve itself in the life of the community. If it has conducted itself well, the church may well have some goodwill in the community, and it is advisable to harness that goodwill to further benefit the community. In this regard, churches should pay attention to how their communities perceive them. One of our partner churches was known by its communities as "the church that cares for people." With this kind of reputation, the community's door is always open to further work.

With this in mind, a great question to ask is, "Where can greater strength be built into the community/communities?" In other words, how can we carry out a software upgrade? For example, how can the church develop people more, as trainers and leaders, but also as holistically as possible? Much community development work, even if unintended, looks at bettering individuals, as shown by the data used to measure progress (e.g. the number of people with access to clean water, the collected stories of individual transformation). But an important question is: How can we move from lifting individuals within communities to regenerating communities? And what mindset changes need to take place to achieve that? The church can also ask: How can we assist the community in building resilience? For example, if there are conflict issues, the church could hold a forum on peace and justice in the light of the pertaining issues. And if the community is lacking drive and seems to be at the mercy of hostile factors, could the church not hold some training on our role as human beings in bringing wholesome development into the world?

How Do We Feel about Our Community?

Another important question we as the church can ask is: How do we feel about our community? What do we value? What do we not like? To help us we can reflect on the pictures of God's intentions for a flourishing community we saw in the biblical story. How do they reflect our community and how do they inspire us to change? Where do we long to see greater integration and renewal? If we consider the longer-term impact and influence of the current projects, we may gain insight into things to build on or gaps to fill.

Does the Church's Mission Have the Right Shape and Balance?

A sensible question to ask in relation to participating in God's larger purposes is: How does the current project sit within the church's overall mission? And equally we can ask: Does the church's mission have the right shape and balance? To help us reflect on these questions, we can ask the following:

- Is Jesus Christ the centre of the mission?
- How is the church reflecting Jesus Christ in truth and love to the world?
- Is the church living as the family of God with different peoples together?

- Is the mission bearing fruit and bringing transformation to the community, spiritually, physically, socially, environmentally and economically?
- Are the poor and needy being lifted up? Are the downtrodden and oppressed becoming free?
- Are young people being inspired to launch new initiatives?
- Is the church participating in the full mission of God?

We need not feel under pressure to achieve more than we are capable of at any one time, but by reflecting on these types of questions we can see what will need adjusting, developing or expanding at some point.

What Are the Next Steps?

We may be able to add value and increase the "software" side concurrently with the project, but the other questions in the other sections are designed for leading us into careful consideration of the next steps for the future. Naturally, it is important to plan these steps well in advance. As part of our deliberations, it may be useful to revisit the results of the listening exercise done for the current project (see chapter 7), see what else was noted then and present it to the Lord for his guidance. There are various categories open to us, which may be considered either individually or in combination:

Completion. We may feel, after good consultation with the participant community, that the current project is approaching completion and has fulfilled many of its objectives. If so, we need to think if and how the participant community will continue. For the church simply to stop its involvement is not a good idea. We may later find things in a state of disuse as unfortunately this is not uncommon with projects after they officially finish. By this stage, the participant community with good ownership should be operating under its own organized and functioning leadership who should be able to ensure that the good work of the project continues to bear fruit. But it would be wise to discuss with the community how they will continue and to confirm that everyone has clear expectations. Checking if any support is needed to ensure a phased finish is essential. At the same time, the church should ask how it will remain relationally involved in the lives of these people through encouragement, prayer and ongoing witness and service. After a celebration of God's goodness this will then also free the church for new opportunities.

Continuation. The church and the community may feel that the current project has been good but has yet to reach its goals, and as such a continuation is the right approach. Maybe the original plan was too optimistic in its expectations. When we think of our progress as disciples of Christ it is often slower than we would have liked. And in terms of seeing the relationships with God, ourselves, others and the rest of creation reconnected and healthy we should be patient. Continuation can be the wise option as it is in the long haul that benefits and impact are seen.

Refinement. Maybe we, the church, together with the community and its leaders have realized that there are deficiencies or gaps that are causing us to miss the transformation the current project was intended to encourage. In this case, together we may need to refine or amend the current project for the next phase. Refinement tends to go with the territory and should be seen as part of the learning process. Everyone can therefore be encouraged to view this positively.

Development. Another category is development in which the next phase is a growth in capacity or features of the existing project. This is common after a pilot project, which has tested the idea in a small and low-risk way, perhaps with a few people, has proved successful. Now is the time to roll it out in a bigger way to more people. Care needs to be taken to ensure the facilitators have the means to oversee matters rather than simply being run off their feet. Another option is to add features or components to the existing project. An example would be to add tree-planting to a conservation agriculture project to promote agroforestry, enhanced agriculture and an increased valuing of the local environment. This encourages participants to think about components in an integrated manner. This developmental approach has the advantage of introducing ideas step by step, building on what has been achieved, rather than overwhelming participants by trying to do many things at once. It is vital that participants learn the value of maintaining what has already been achieved and developing new ideas so that the former is not just abandoned in pursuit of the latter.

Expansion. At some point the church will be ready for a larger expansion, either by adding significant dimensions to be integrated with an existing project or by beginning a completely new missional venture. To decide that this is the right course of action it is likely we will have seen good fruit in our current integral mission projects and have established some good local relationships and capabilities to the extent that we have a humble confidence in God to proceed. For us, after working a few years with our church in Tanzania in several of its congregations across the region to facilitate conservation agriculture, together we saw the opportunity for something new. While many participants were enjoying flourishing fields and better harvests, for two of the villages there was particular environmental destruction through the excessive cutting down of trees and always much less rainfall. The whole region was being impacted by climate change due at least partially to environmental degradation through deforestation, nomadic pastoralism and bad farming practices, all influenced by both physical and spiritual factors. Consequently, we all realized the need to do something more comprehensive and conceived of the communities' integrated renewal project encompassing and combining conservation agriculture, tree-planting, beekeeping, livestock, business, evangelism and discipleship. The inspiration came from reflecting on Ezekiel 36:22–36, the stunning passage outlined in chapter 2 where God promises to renew his people and transform their land *with the result* that the nations will know he is God.[4] Could this passage, which in many ways epitomizes the transformation this current book envisages, be enacted again?

Planting a New Church?

We saw in our survey of the book of Acts and the New Testament epistles that church planting was an intrinsic part of the early church's evangelistic and missional strategy. And yet we have not considered church planting . . . until now! Churches and church denominations in Africa are usually church-planting movements and this is a cause of celebration. The question is, can integral mission be harnessed with church planting? I believe so. Churches that have successfully embraced and carried out integral mission in their locality may be especially ripe for seeing the opportunity to begin a new church plant in a new location, as part of their being captured by God's larger purpose and wider mission. In this section I will offer a few thoughts around the possibility of planting a church as the appropriate next stage of further carrying out integral mission and being a channel for community development.

Why Are We Interested in Planting a New Church?

The first question to consider is: *Why* are we interested in planting a new church? What is our motivation? We need to be honest with ourselves. If our

---

4. Skip Krige, imploring the integration of discipleship, evangelism and community development, says, "We need churches *connected to God's heart and*, at the same time, to *the cries of the people*. We need churches that will *combine evangelism with economic empowerment*, and *discipleship with community development . . . empowered communities* that will usher in new and restored neighbourhoods." ("Towards a Coherent Vision for Faith-Based Development," *Journal of Theology for Southern Africa* 132 [Nov. 2008]: 31.)

reason is to grow the denomination or satisfy our ego, then planting another church will probably be a bad idea. We may simply "steal sheep" from other churches. And how empty is that! But if our motivation is God's glory and kingdom, because we desire to see Jesus's cosmic reconciliation extended and we ache to see the poor experiencing God's love and being lifted up, then maybe God is directing us. We may also have gifted church members who need the space to lead a new initiative. We must, though, be attentive to God's voice and see if he is calling us. Let our motive, if God is calling us, be to plant a *significant and community-transforming church.*

Where Should We Plant a New Church?

The second question is: *Where* should we plant a new church? This is a huge topic and we cannot offer a complete answer here; we simply give some pointers to consider with prayerful reflection as the church seeks to discern God's leading. It is vital to explore whether there is a genuine need for a new church in the locality under consideration. Remember, Paul's concern was to take the gospel to new places, among different and *unreached* peoples. He writes to the Romans,

> Yet I have written to you quite boldly on some points to remind you of them again, because of the grace God gave me to be a minister of Christ Jesus to the Gentiles. He gave me the priestly duty of proclaiming the gospel of God, so that the Gentiles might become an offering acceptable to God, sanctified by the Holy Spirit.
>
> Therefore I glory in Christ Jesus in my service to God. I will not venture to speak of anything except what Christ has accomplished through me in leading the Gentiles to obey God by what I have said and done – by the power of signs and wonders, through the power of the Spirit of God. So from Jerusalem all the way round to Illyricum, I have fully proclaimed the gospel of Christ. It has always been my ambition to preach the gospel where Christ was not known, so that I would not be building on someone else's foundation. (Rom 15:15–20)

We see that integral mission was part of Paul's gospel strategy, presenting the gospel in word and deed, and in life too, he adds in 1 Thessalonians 2:8. He writes Romans in part to have the Roman church be a support for his mission to Spain where "Christ was not known" (Rom 15:20, 24). Coupled with this church-planting ministry for Paul was his social concern for the poor (Rom 15:23–29). While the context was the poor Christian brothers and sisters in Jerusalem, it was all part of demonstrating the credibility of the gospel. The church was an extended family of different peoples united in Christ and thus a visual expression of the gospel (Gal 3:28). We should therefore see a concern for the poor, inside and by extension outside the church, as a disclosure of the gospel and hence intrinsic to worthwhile church planting. Let us look for the communities in desperate need – with spiritual, physical, economic, communal and environmental needs.

How Should We Plant the New Church?

The third question is: *How* should we plant the church? To answer this, we can utilize the sections of chapter 7 about how to design a suitable project now in a larger way for how to proceed in planting a church, and chapter 6 about integrating the missional tasks into a unified outreach. The new church will gain credibility more quickly if it shows concern for the community's total need. It would be a mistake simply to use the same method employed in establishing the mother church, for example. Each context is different and it is wise to approach the new church-planting venture with humility, openness and flexibility, especially looking for the paths into the community. I remember visiting a pastor and his wife who had planted a church seven years previously in an overwhelmingly Muslim community. By then the church had only grown to thirteen members and none were former Muslims. Everyone was a "visitor" who had come to the area for business. We asked the pastor what his evangelistic approach was and he replied, "I use open-air meetings." Sadly, they served only to drive the community from the church and the pastor and his wife to despondency. When we enquired about the make-up of the community and what they did, he answered, "They are all subsistence farmers." Maybe a better approach could have included a building of relationships with community members through conservation agriculture and enabling them to increase their crop yields, thus demonstrating the goodness of God.

One final point: if a new church plant is to acquire land, it may be advisable to try to obtain a sufficient piece of land that the church can use for projects for community transformation rather than simply for worship services alone.

Conclusion

God's mission is always bigger than any missional endeavour that we have done so far. This should be a healthy provocation for us to seek to partner with him more deeply and more widely, as we draw on the words of Ephesians 3:20–21, "*Now to him who is able to do immeasurably more than all we ask or imagine, according to his power that is at work within us, to him be glory in the church and in Christ Jesus throughout all generations, for ever and ever! Amen.*" So in this chapter we have explored some of the ways in which we can move on from our initial project into God's larger purpose and wider mission, which include:

- ensure a people-centred approach
- prayerfully dwell in the biblical narrative
- keep our ear close to the ground to the voices of the community
- ask wise questions: how to add value, how greater strength can be built into the community, how we feel about our community, and how is the shape of the church's current missional engagement
- determine the next steps: continuation, refinement, development or expansion?
- consider whether it is appropriate to plant a new transforming church in a new location

These, therefore, are some ideas whereby we can be captured by and participate in the larger arena of God's mission. In our closing chapter I take this further by considering Jesus and exploring how the church, rooted and built up in him, might continue to live out his transforming mission.

10

A God-Filled and God-Like Church among Its Community

Transforming Church: God Has Been among Us!

We have seen our immense privilege and responsibility as the church to be involved with God in his transforming work in the world. We have considered in detail how often the church must be reconfigured in its outlook, life and mission to be fit for purpose so as to partner well with God in this tremendous work. Indeed, it is an ongoing process of being reshaped and revitalized, by surrendering to God and allowing him to work in us. I cannot underestimate the significance of our being moulded and remoulded by the Living God for his missional purposes.

We have also considered what God's transformation looks like, a transformation of the vital relationships of communities whereby communities flourish in all respects, with the church through the Spirit as the sign, instrument and foretaste of this transformation. It is important we do not get carried away by utopian ideals, thinking that we can, by our own efforts, bring them to fruition. We must always be guided by God's vision of kingdom transformation, a vision which is both *now* and *not yet*, and which only he can execute but in his mercy involves us in. The fact is that transformation is not always possible and we should not "over-expect" or overpromise in our efforts. And yet communities usually do not expect all their troubles to vanish. They must, though, be allowed to enjoy the measure of transformation they experience, a transformation which might not be as we imagined.

Even though suffering and hardship will sadly remain, we are called to play our role faithfully in God's mission, to enter into that suffering and point beyond it to the goodness of God. There are two questions I wish to explore further in this chapter: How can we, the church, join communities in their life journey so they see God and exclaim, "God has been among us?" And how can we be enabled to integrate community development organically within the overall life and mission of the church? If we can answer these questions and do them, then we may become "Transforming Church"! The following story approaches these questions practically.

God Continues to Work after the Project, Bringing Unexpected Fruit!

Ezekiel's hot and dusty Magozi village in the East African Rift Valley was where we began. Yes, we were asked to facilitate a new church-led fuel-efficient stoves project, but more than that we were participating in God's mission. It was this passage that inspired us: "The Word became flesh and blood, and moved into the neighborhood. We saw the glory with our own eyes, the one-of-a-kind glory, like Father, like Son, generous inside and out, true from start to finish" (John 1:14 *The Message*). We knew we needed to live with the people and move into their world. It would not be about visiting once a week to offer training: we wanted to be part of the church and community and do life together. So we rented an ordinary house in the centre of the village a stone's throw from the local church. And we began our first faltering steps. We walked, we visited, we sat, we ate, we talked. And we were generously received. It was mission and life together. We joined the line at the tap with our buckets to collect water and played football with the children on the sandy ground. We cooked outside as villagers stood, watched and wondered what we were going to eat. We worked, studied the Bible and prayed together. Invited to preach in the church services and share in the evangelistic outreach, we conveyed God's heart that all might believe in his Son Jesus and receive the right to become his children and receive life. And most of all, we saw God together.

But after seven years and having moved a thousand kilometres away, we visited again – what would we see? Well, the hospitality had not diminished but grown – three big lunches that day! But more than that, the seeds God had sown through his presence and prayer, his word and his vision had grown into a tree with different kinds of fruit – as our former neighbour Rose put it – which they were still picking. The fruit was far beyond anything we had imagined. We listened as various villagers shared what had happened. The Ebenezer stoves group (as they called themselves) were still continuing with the project, but using profits to begin other businesses, buy two plots of land and even a tractor jointly owned. Rose talked about how the group had just picked the "tractor fruit" and would now look for the next fruit ready to be picked! They were about to begin a tree-planting initiative, supported by our colleagues Jesca and Ibrahimu. Another shared his gratitude for the education given them that they still possessed and which was far more valuable than money, which would have long gone without leaving a mark. The lady who had cried on receiving a Bible seven years previously now proclaimed, "Poverty is finished!" By others' standards her poverty might have remained to some extent, but her view was the standard that mattered.

Lucas shared about the physical and spiritual help that was given through the group. He proudly presented his miracle child. Seven years before we and others had prayed with him and his wife who was unable to conceive. Little Kathryn was now a strapping five-year-old! A father shared about the learned importance of family and teaching children. Ezekiel read from 2 Corinthians 4:7, sharing how people had mocked them in the beginning for playing with dirt, but in truth God had made and moulded us all as clay. "We have a treasure in jars of clay that is shining out, and now people in the village see that this clay has led to other things," he declared. The church had indeed grown and was thriving. I recalled the pastor's impassioned preaching, as the project began, that the church was called to be salt and light, and I thought, "Yes, it is true here." The deposit placed by God had indeed yielded a great transformation, one that was still unfinished and ongoing. It was all God's work, and he deserved all the praise!

"God Has Been among Us": Jesus, the Church and God's Mission

That story certainly whets our appetite and opens our eyes to what God can do. I return to our two posed questions: How can we, the church, join communities in their life journey so they see God and exclaim, "God has been among us?" And how can we be enabled to integrate community development organically within the overall life and mission of the church? I shall reflect on these questions further, this time by exploring Jesus, the church and God's mission in John's gospel. *This gospel beautifully displays the mission of God enacted in Jesus the Son, which is now to be carried forward by the church as a community in Jesus through the power of the Spirit.* Jesus is the one who pioneers the fulfilling of God's mission and then after his resurrection commissions his disciples, "As the Father has sent me, even so I am sending you" (John 20:21 ESV; cf. 17:18). The words "as" and "even so" explain to us that we are to approach mission *in the same way* Jesus does. Therefore, let us first look at Jesus, his mission and the manner in which he accomplishes this mission, before then using this to reflect on the church's mission and how it should be conducted.

Jesus, the Messianic King and Tabernacling Presence of God among the People

John begins his gospel in the most profound way, giving us a new set of glasses so that we can see: "In the beginning was the Word, and the Word was with God, and the Word was God. He was with God in the beginning" (John 1:1).

We see the uniqueness of Jesus's *being* and of his eternal relationship with God, and hence how the impact of his coming is to be like no other! Not only does Jesus have "cosmic significance" at the outset of the gospel, but we are told "what will be of primary importance in the rest of its story – the issue of Jesus' identity in relation to that of God."[1]

As the Word (Gk. *logos*), Jesus creates, reveals, delivers and brings life and meaning. And through him beneficial order is achieved in the universe. There is no revelation, salvation, life or meaning outside him. As we saw in chapter 3, the phrase "in the beginning" also evokes the opening words of Genesis and sets the coming of Jesus in the context of God's whole story of the world. Indeed, John in his opening eighteen verses retells this story with Jesus's coming into the world as entering the story at the crisis point to bring it to its rightful climax, the new creation, in which those who receive him enjoy life as children of God. The remainder of John 1 through to John 2:11 witnesses to the first week of God's new creation.[2] Such is the work of Jesus the Word!

If we ask how we can move from our brokenness and the brokenness of this world to possessing this status as God's children (1:12) in the new creation, the answer comes spectacularly in verse 14: "The Word became flesh and made his dwelling among us. We have seen his glory, the glory of the one and only Son, who came from the Father, full of grace and truth." John 1:14 is the verse that unlocks the whole of John's gospel. Stunningly, the One who is the Word, who was with God in the beginning, who is God, and who is life and the true light, has not stood back afar watching and waiting, but has become a human being and jumped in the middle of the "crocodile-infested" waters and saved us. Jesus entered this creation – *the Word became a human being*[3] – lived with us and revealed God's glory.

---

1. Andrew Lincoln, *The Gospel According to St. John*, Black's New Testament Commentaries (New York: Continuum, 2005), 93.

2. Day 1: John the Baptist prepares the way for the new exodus (1:19–28); Day 2: The witness of John the Baptist (1:29–34); Day 3: The witness of the first disciples (1:35–42); Day 4: The witness of Philip and Nathanael (1:43–51); Day 7: Jesus's own witness at the wedding of Cana (2:1–11). (1:29, 35 and 43 each begin with "On the next day" and 2:1 begins with jumping to "On the third day," which show that the events recorded in 1:19 – 2:11 all occur in 7 days.)

3. This highlights that God's word is best seen through being lived out.

The word translated as "dwelling" means that he "pitched his tent" or "tabernacled" among us. This picks up the exodus – the great time in Israel's history when God dwelled with his people displaying his awesome presence and power. Moses had constructed a tabernacle as a sanctuary whereby God could live among his people as they journeyed from the land of slavery, through the mighty Red Sea, on to Mount Sinai and finally to the promised land. Throughout, God himself lived with his people, guiding them in the pillar of cloud by day and the pillar of fire by night.

Jesus's coming is like the time of the exodus. God has come to live with his people in power, but this time he has come in person. Jesus's coming as the tabernacling presence of God is about his taking us to the new creation through a new exodus. In the first exodus, God delivered his people and revealed his glory. This time the deliverance is available to all peoples, to leave the horrible results of sin – slavery, oppression, ruined lives – and become the free children of God. In the incarnation, God becomes what we are in order that we can become like he is.

Later the temple replaced the tabernacle as God's dwelling place among his people, the place of meeting with God for both Israel and the nations, the place of finding life, wholeness and forgiveness, and the place from which life flows out into the barren places and brings transformation. The theme of temple has rightly been recognized by Africans as significant for understanding Jesus in John's gospel.[4] *Jesus is the new temple* (2:12–22) and is the fulfilment of the various feasts or festivals celebrated at the Jerusalem temple.[5] What was therefore once available through the temple is now fully available through Jesus. His mission can thus be correctly understood as a *temple-mission*, and what makes this mission viable is his vital connection with God and his vital connection with humanity.

John also points out in his opening that Jesus, the Word made flesh, is the Christ or Messiah (1:17) and God's Son (1:18). As Messiah, Jesus is the long-awaited anointed King who as God's Son would reign on David's throne over a worldwide kingdom (2 Sam 7; 1 Chr 28–29; Pss 2; 72; Isa 9:6–7). John is particularly keen to unveil a profound portrayal of Jesus's identity and within that to explore the nature of his messiahship. In the opening chapter, Jesus is

---

4. E.g. see Mzayifani H. Mzebetshana and Annang Asumang, "Temple Christology in the Gospel According to John: A Survey of Scholarship in the Last Twenty Years (1996–2016)," *Conspectus* (Sep. 2017): 133–63.

5. In structuring his account of Jesus, John shows particular concern for how Jesus fulfils these feasts: Passover (2:12 – 4:54), an unnamed festival (5:1–47), Passover (6:1–71), Tabernacles (7:1 – 10:21) and the Festival of Dedication (10:22 – 12:50).

revealed as Messiah, Son of God and Davidic King (1:26–27, 31–34, 41, 45, 49).[6] It is the fact that Jesus is "in the closest relationship with the Father" or "at the Father's side" (1:18) which enables his kingship to be both so powerful and a true expression of God's own kingship as being full of grace and truth; his mission then is also a *kingdom-mission*. Throughout this gospel, we see Jesus's determination to accomplish the Father's will (2:17; 4:34; 5:17; 6:38–39; 7:17; 9:4; 17:4). His presence and his powerful words and deeds are also God's own presence and kingdom (5:19; 12:49). But his kingship, based on his being God's Son, is also a clear redefining of Jewish expectations to include suffering. It is in his arrest and trial that he is acclaimed as king (18:33, 37, 39; 19:3, 12, 14, 15) and in his crucifixion and death he is enthroned as king (19:19, 21; cf. 12:13, 15). His kingship is not for his own sake, but by his submitting to the will of his Father it is for the sake of humanity.

What makes Jesus function both as temple and king is his *oneness* with God the Father (10:30). Jesus through his presence, life, words and deeds – his whole mission – has made the invisible God now visible (1:18). To see Jesus is to see God. Through Jesus's life and mission, seamlessly woven together – his integral mission – people experience God's presence and gracious rule. As a man of God, he is also a man of the people!

Jesus beautifully lives out the essence of temple and kingdom, so naturally connected to the people in daily life, and pointing forward to the day when the whole world will be God's temple and kingdom, full of his life and presence (cf. Gen 1). He displays the glory and generosity of God at a wedding (John 2:1–11), he explains eternal life to someone who comes to him at night (3:1–21), and when tired at the end of a journey he engages with and offers true life to a marginalized Samaritan woman who then becomes a powerful evangelist to her town (4:1–42). He brings dramatic healings no one thought possible to a royal official's child and a man with long-term disabilities (4:43–54; 5:1–16), as well as showing his power over creation and making amazing holistic provision for a crowd, with more food left at the end than they had at the beginning (6:1–71). In the middle of a festival Jesus issues the invitation to receive the life-giving water of the Spirit (7:25–44), grants uncalled-for grace and truth (7:53 – 8:11) and physical and spiritual light (8:12 – 9:41), and reveals that he is the Good Shepherd of the people, putting their needs before his own

---

6. See Beth Stovell, "Son of God as Anointed One? Johannine Davidic Christology and Second Temple Messianism," in *Reading the Gospel of John's Christology as Jewish Messianism: Royal, Prophetic, and Divine Messiahs*, eds. Benjamin Reynolds and Gabriele Boccaccini (Leiden: Brill, 2018), 151–77.

(10:1–21). He both weeps with the bereaved, entering their pain, and having prayed raises the dead to life (11:1–44). And Jesus, amid hostility and plots against him, shows that his glory is to give his life as a kernel of wheat for the greater life of the whole world (12:20–50).

We therefore see Jesus, the life, bringing the multifaceted life of God. "This life is holistic and abundant, both 'spiritual' and material – an embodied wholeness"[7] – personal, communal, creational. His work is "life-giving in the fullest sense of the word, addressing spiritual, emotional, physical, economic, and other human needs."[8]

John shows us that Jesus's mission is the Father's mission, which is to give life, creating children of God with his life and likeness who share in the Father-Son mission to the world. And so, after his resurrection, Jesus meeting the disciples says, "As the Father has sent me, I am sending you" (20:21). He prefaces this with "Peace be with you!" and follows by breathing on them and saying, "Receive the Holy Spirit. If you forgive anyone's sins, their sins are forgiven; if you do not forgive them, they are not forgiven" (20:22–23). They receive his peace and are to extend it; namely "the wholeness and the harmony associated with God's coming kingdom, which begins with forgiveness of the people's sins."[9] It is therefore in many ways a new "Genesis" mission, this time empowered by the Holy Spirit (picking up Gen 2:7), who joins us to God's mission.

A God-Filled and God-Like Church among Its Community

Jesus has blazed a trail for us as the church in our mission. Surely it is just a case of emulating or copying him and launching out on our mission? Well, the disciples in John 21, in a passage that likely symbolizes the mission of the church, show that it is not quite that easy, as they fish all night without catching a thing! But when they are attentive to his words "Throw your net on the right side of the boat" (21:6), it is a different story. So let us look at a better way.

Before giving his disciples this commission (20:21), Jesus spends his last night with them before his crucifixion preparing them with his "mission discourse"[10] (John 13–17). They are founded as "his own" people (13:1; cf.

---

7. Michael Gorman, *Abide and Go: Missional Theosis in the Gospel of John*, The Didsbury Lecture Series (Eugene, OR: Cascade, 2018), 182.

8. Gorman, *Abide and Go*, 190.

9. Gorman, 137.

10. Gorman, 77.

1:10), to be like him, following his extreme servant example and being marked by love for one another, that the world might know that they are his disciples (13:34–35). Mission and community go hand in hand since, as Gorman says, "Christian mission naturally creates community, and a healthy Christian community naturally creates mission."[11] What is important for us in following Jesus in mission is not that we simply try to emulate him. Rather, he empowers us by continuing to be present with us through his sending of the Spirit. Jesus says, "You will realise that I am in my Father, and you are in me, and I am in you" (14:20). Without participating in the very life of God we could not possibly succeed. It is sometimes recognized that our mutual dwelling with Jesus points to the church-with-Jesus as a temple, full of the presence of God and ready to be expanded.[12] This may hint at how the-Word-made-flesh will continue to tabernacle and reveal God's glory to the world.

John 15–16 is about life as the new humanity – a life intimately connected to Jesus, and with the Spirit who enables the church to live in and testify to an opposing world. First, the temple becomes the vine. Jesus is the true vine[13] and we are the branches. We are to remain in him, allowing his life to flow into us (15:1–8). This is all for the purpose that we might "go and bear fruit" (15:16) as his life flows through us to others. We bear the fruit of mission by *remaining in Jesus* – not by our independent efforts – as a loving united church community connected to him. In this way, there is no contradiction between "remain" and "go," since we go and bear fruit as we remain in Jesus through love and obedience. Second, the Spirit will operate as the Spirit of truth in the life of the church so that the church witnesses about Jesus to its surrounding community (16:7–15).

As we live this empowered way as a people in the midst of our community, they will see the greater works of Jesus and the glory of God, and will experience his eternal life: namely, "that they know you, the only true God, and Jesus Christ, whom you have sent" (17:3). Jesus, in chapter 17, gathers up in prayer the concerns of chapters 13–16: that as the church increasingly finds itself in God, casting other agendas aside, it will grow together as one, becoming a people in the world but not of the world (17:20–23). We will live out our calling "as both a reconciled and a reconciling community, to share the peace

---

11. Gorman, 193.

12. Mary Coloe, "Dwelling in the Household of God. Jn 14:2," in *That Our Joy May Be Complete: Essays on the Incarnation for the New Millennium*, eds. Marian Free, Rosemary Gill, Jonathan Holland and John Mainstone (Adelaide: Openbook, 2000), 47–57.

13. The vine was a symbol of Israel (Ps 80:8–18; Hos 10:1–2; Isa 5:1–7; Jer 2:21).

and restoration [we] have received."[14] We will be a growing temple, centred in the Triune God and participating in the kingdom that is not from this world but is for this world (18:33).

This is the beauty of mission when we see it this way. Jesus not only sends us; he comes with us, ensuring that our mission is effective. It is Jesus-present, Jesus-dependent and Jesus-empowered mission. We can see where he is working, doing what the Father does, and join in. We will not, like the disciples, try to fish apart from Jesus! This is such an encouragement for the church, so as to be a community embodying the message, to be so connected to God and at the same time so connected to its surrounding community. *People need to see a God-filled church, bearing his likeness, truly among its community.* As the church becomes this, the community will experience God among them (Immanuel) in compassion, challenge and confrontation. They will encounter the tabernacling presence of God and the kingdom of God all at once. People will experience the church journeying with them, displaying true humanity, especially in their struggles and pain, so they see heaven open, catching sight of a loving God and being invited into his reign.[15]

The Jesus of John 2–12 can be seen again, this time through the church. Instead of allowing our mission to be programme-based, it will be life-based. As we become more immersed in the life of our community, they will see through us the abundance of God at community events, God's love for the world, his spiritual and physical living water to the outcasts without judgement, mighty works of life-giving power among the forgotten, and miraculous provision in desperate places. They will hear the words of eternal life and see the light of life – in teaching, answered prayer and grace – and they will know that the Good Shepherd is with them through us his under-shepherds, a people who offer our lives for the community to experience resurrection life, the life of the new creation. Thus, we will bear fruit that will last in Jesus-shaped mission. And the church will faithfully embody the good news of Jesus, telling – in life, word and deed – the whole story from creation to new creation, and people in the community will believe that "Jesus is the Messiah, the Son of God, and . . . by believing [they] may have life in his name" (20:30–31). They will see a better, transforming story!

In this way, *the life of an incarnated missional church provides the right setting for community development.* Our community development activities will

---

14. Gorman, *Abide and Go*, 137.

15. This is what Jesus promises Nathanael when he says, "You will see 'heaven open, and the angels of God ascending and descending on' the Son of Man" (John 1:51).

be properly embedded in our life and mission as the church. These activities will find their proper context, demonstrating the truth of John 3:16 and contributing to bearing the lasting fruit of the gospel. Our mission will not be a switch we turn on or off – it will always be on. The image of God as renewed by Jesus will be displayed to others through *who* we are and *what* and *how* we tell and do. There will be a beautiful blending of proclamation, witness, service, justice, reconciliation and development, providing communities with a foretaste of the joyful shalom that God will one day bring fully to earth. And together, we and our communities will glimpse a fresh view of the Living God and know that he is among us.

Conclusion

The African church has, as we have seen, the resources to participate in God's mission through community development. These resources come from the Triune God himself and they enable the church as it lives in God to approach its missional endeavours biblically, theologically, culturally and practically to share with him in bringing his transforming work in all spheres of life to Africa's communities. May God be with the church in Africa, may he inspire its imagination, and may he use it mightily among its communities for his kingdom and glory.

Bibliography

Ajulu, Deborah. "Development as Holistic Mission." In *Holistic Mission: God's Plan for God's People*, Edinburgh Centenary 5, edited by Brian Woolnough and Wonsuk Ma, 160–174. Oxford: Regnum, 2010.

Arnold, Bill T. *Genesis*. NCBC. New York: CUP, 2008.

Beasley-Murray, George R. *John*. Word Biblical Commentary 36. Nashville: Thomas Nelson, 1987.

Best, Ernest. *Ephesians*. International Critical Commentary. Edinburgh: Bloomsbury T&T Clark, 1998.

Bloomfield, Steve. *Africa United: How Football Explains Africa*. Edinburgh: Canongate, 2011.

Boaheng, Isaac. *Poverty, the Bible, and Africa: Contextual Foundations for Helping the Poor*. Carlisle: HippoBooks, 2020. Kindle.

Bosch, David J. *Transforming Mission: Paradigm Shifts in Theology of Mission*. Maryknoll: Orbis, 1991.

Carson, D. A., ed. *NIV Zondervan Study Bible*. Grand Rapids: Zondervan, 2015.

Chester, Tim. "Introducing Integral Mission." In Chester, *Justice, Mercy and Humility*, 1–11.

Chester, Tim, ed. *Justice, Mercy and Humility: Integral Mission and the Poor*. Carlisle: Paternoster, 2002.

Chike, Chigoe. "Proudly African, Proudly Christian: The Roots of Christologies in the African Worldview." *Black Theology* 6, no. 2 (May 2008): 221–40.

Clines, D. J. A. "The Image of God in Man." *Tyndale Bulletin* 19 (1968): 53–103.

Coloe, Mary. "Dwelling in the Household of God. Jn 14:2," in *That Our Joy May Be Complete: Essays on the Incarnation for the New Millennium*, edited by Marian Free, Rosemary Gill, Jonathan Holland and John Mainstone, 47–57. Adelaide: Openbook, 2000.

Corbett, Steve, and Brian Fikkert. *When Helping Hurts: How to Alleviate Poverty without Hurting the Poor . . . and Yourself*. Second edition. Chicago: Moody, 2012.

Duggan, C. S. M. "Doing Bad by Doing Good? Theft and Abuse by Lenders in the Microfinance Markets of Uganda." *Studies in Comparative International Development* 51 (2016): 189–208.

Dumbrell, William. *Covenant and Creation: A Theology of Old Testament Covenants*. Nashville: Thomas Nelson, 1984.

Flemming, Dean. *Contextualization in the New Testament: Patterns for Theology and Mission*. Leicester: Apollos, 2005.

———. *Recovering the Full Mission of God: A Biblical Perspective on Being, Doing and Telling*. Downers Grove: InterVarsity Press 2013. Kindle.

Fountain, Dan, ed. *Let's Restore Our Land*. Fort Myers: Echo, 2007.

George, Sherron. "God's Holistic Mission: Fullness of Parts, Participants, and Places." *Missiology: An International Review* 41, no. 3 (2013): 286–99.

Goheen, Michael W. *Introducing Christian Mission Today: Scripture, History and Issues*. Downers Grove: IVP Academic, 2014.

Gorman, Michael. *Abide and Go: Missional Theosis in the Gospel of John*. The Didsbury Lecture Series. Eugene: Cascade, 2018.

———. *Becoming the Gospel: Paul, Participation and Mission*. Grand Rapids: Eerdmans, 2015.

Grant, Jamie A., and Dewi A. Hughes. *Transforming the World? The Gospel and Social Responsibility*. Nottingham: Apollos, 2009.

Greer, Peter. *Entrepreneurship for Human Flourishing*. Washington, DC: AEI Press, 2014.

Greer, Peter, and Chris Horst. *Mission Drift: The Unspoken Crisis Facing Leaders, Charities and Churches*. Minneapolis: Bethany House, 2014.

Hastings, Ross. *Missional God, Missional Church: Hope for Re-evangelising the West*. Downers Grove: IVP Academic, 2012.

Healey, Joseph, and Donald Sybertz. *Towards an African Narrative Theology*. Maryknoll: Orbis, 1996.

Imasogi, Osadolor. "The Church and Theological Ferment in Africa." *Review & Expositor* 82, no. 2 (Spring 1985): 225–36.

Kalu, Ogbu U. "Preserving a Worldview: Pentecostalism in the African Maps of the Universe." *Pneuma: The Journal of the Society for Pentecostal Studies* 24, no. 2 (Fall 2002): 110–37.

Katongole, Emmanuel. *The Sacrifice of Africa: A Political Theology for Africa*. Grand Rapids: Eerdmans, 2011.

Klobodu, Seth Selorm, Sarah Kessner and Levi Johnson. "Africa Is on the Verge of a Major Health Crisis and the Need for Nutrition and Health Surveys Is Imperative." *The Pan African Medical Journal* 30 (2018): 173. https://www.ncbi.nlm.nih.gov/pmc/articles/PMC6235492/.

Krige, Skip. "Towards a Coherent Vision for Faith-Based Development." *Journal of Theology for Southern Africa* 132 (Nov. 2008): 16–37.

Kunhiyop, Samuel Waje. *African Christian Theology*. Grand Rapids: Zondervan Academic, 2012. Kindle.

Leeming, David A. *Creation Myths of the World: An Encyclopedia*. Vol. 1. Second edition. Santa Barbara: ABC-Clio, 2010.

Lincoln, Andrew. *The Gospel According to St. John*. Black's New Testament Commentaries. New York: Continuum, 2005.

Mallett, Rich, Teddy Atim and Jimmy Opio. "'Bad Work' and the Challenges of Creating Decent Work for Youth in Northern Uganda." Secure Livelihoods Research Consortium, Briefing Paper 25 (Mar. 2017). https://securelivelihoods.org/wp-content/uploads/%E2%80%98Bad-work%E2%80%99-and-the-challenges-of-creating-decent-work-for-youth-in-northern-Uganda.pdf.

Mbiti, John. *African Religions and Philosophy*. 2nd edition. Oxford: Heinemann, 1989.

———. "God, Sin, and Salvation in African Religion." *The Journal of the Interdenominational Theological Center* 16, no. 1–2 (Fall 1988–Spring 1989): 59–68.

Mburu, Elizabeth. *African Hermeneutics*. Carlisle: HippoBooks, 2019.

McAffee, Lauren Green, and Michael McAfee. "The Bible's Impact on Human Rights." *Christianity Today* online, 28 June 2019. https://www.christianitytoday.com/ct/2019/june-web-only/not-what-you-think-michael-lauren-mcafee.html.

McClymond, Kathryn, Julius H. Bailey, Robert André LaFleur and Grant L. Voth, *Great Mythologies of the World*. Chantilly: The Teaching Company, 2015.

Monger, Timothy J. "An East African Perspective on Jesus as Revealer of the Father through His Use of the Friend at Midnight Parable as a Means for Teaching Powerful Prayer (Luke 11:1–13)." In Reed and Ngaruiya, *Who Do You Say I Am?*, 25–42.

Monger, Timothy J., and Marco Methuselah. "God's Masterpiece: Ephesians 2:11–22 as Inspiration for the Church's Involvement in Peacemaking and Reconciliation with People with Albinism in Tanzania." In Reed and Ngaruiya, *Forgiveness, Peacemaking and Reconciliation*, 103–26.

Musau, Zipporah. "Africa Grapples with Huge Disparities in Education." *Africa Renewal*, December 2017–March 2018. https://www.un.org/africarenewal/magazine/december-2017-march-2018/africa-grapples-huge-disparities-education.

Myers, Bryant L. "Progressive Pentecostalism, Development, and Christian Development NGOs: A Challenge and an Opportunity." *International Bulletin of Missionary Research* 39, no. 3 (Jul. 2015): 115–20.

———. *Walking with the Poor: Principles and Practices of Transformational Development*. Revised and expanded edition. Maryknoll: Orbis, 2011.

Mzebetshana, Mzayifani H., and Annang Asumang. "Temple Christology in the Gospel According to John: A Survey of Scholarship in the Last Twenty Years (1996–2016)." *Conspectus* (Sep. 2017): 133–63.

Nicolaci, Marida. "Divine Kingship and Jesus's Identity in Johannine Messianism." In *Reading the Gospel of John's Christology as Jewish Messianism: Royal, Prophetic, and Divine Messiahs*, edited by Benjamin Reynolds and Gabriele Boccaccini, 178–202. Leiden: Brill, 2018.

Nordstokke, Kjell. "Faith-Based Organisations (FBOs) and Their Distinct Assets." *Swedish Missiological Themes* 101, no. 2 (2013): 185–202.

Nyamiti, Charles. "Contemporary Liberation Theologies in the Light of the African Traditional Conception of Evil." *Studia Missionalia* 45 (1996): 237–65.

Otijele, P. Yakubu. "Understanding the African Worldview: A Religious Perspective." *Ogbomoso Journal of Theology* (6 Dec. 1991): 1–16.

Padilla, C. René. "Integral Mission and Its Historical Development." In Chester, *Justice, Mercy and Humility*, 42–58.

Poncian, Japhace, and Edward S. Mgaya. "Africa's Leadership Challenges in the 21st Century: What Can Leaders Learn from Africa's Pre-Colonial Leadership and Governance?" *International Journal of Social Science Studies* 3, no. 3 (May 2015): 106–15.

President of the Republic of Kenya. "Proclamation of the National Day of Prayer by H. E. Uhuru Kenyatta, C.G.H., President of the Republic of Kenya and Commander-in-Chief of the Defence Forces, 17th March 2020." https://www.president.go.ke/2020/03/17/proclamation-of-the-national-day-of-prayer-by-h-e-uhuru-kenyatta-c-g-h-president-of-the-republic-of-kenya-and-commander-in-chief-of-the-defence-forces-17th-march-2020/?fbclid=IwAR1Q4x6_5abqSG6NWuIc6iH35CO7dbAXP4zETp7itgE3UyiD7qVEWu-WL3o.

Reed, Rodney, and Gift Mtukwa. "Christ Our Ancestor: African Christology and the Danger of Contextualization." *Wesleyan Theological Journal* 45, no. 1 (Spring 2010): 144–63.

Reed, Rodney L., and David K. Ngaruiya, eds. *Forgiveness, Peacemaking and Reconciliation.* Africa Society of Evangelical Theology Series 5. Carlisle: Langham Global Library, 2020.

———. *Who Do You Say I Am? Christology in Africa.* Africa Society of Evangelical Theology Series 6. Carlisle: Langham Global Library, 2021.

Ringma, Charles. "Holistic Ministry and Mission: A Call for Reconceptualization." *Missiology: An International Review* 32, no. 4 (Oct. 2004): 431–48.

Ryken, Leland, et al., eds. *Dictionary of Biblical Imagery.* Downers Grove: InterVarsity Press 1998.

Smart, Jessica. "What Is Community Development?" Australian Institute of Family Studies (AIFS). Updated 2019. https://aifs.gov.au/resources/practice-guides/what-community-development.

Stinton, Diane B. *Jesus of Africa: Voices of Contemporary Africa Christology.* Maryknoll: Orbis, 2004.

Stovell, Beth. "Son of God as Anointed One? Johannine Davidic Christology and Second Temple Messianism." In *Reading the Gospel of John's Christology as Jewish Messianism: Royal, Prophetic, and Divine Messiahs,* edited by Benjamin Reynolds and Gabriele Boccaccini, 151–77. Leiden: Brill, 2018.

Tallack, Barney. "5 Existential Funding Challenges for Large INGOs." Bond, 2 July 2020. "https://www.bond.org.uk/news/2020/07/5-existential-funding-challenges-for-large-ingos.

350Africa.org. "8 Ways Climate Change Is Already Affecting Africa." Accessed 29 July 2022. https://350africa.org/8-ways-climate-change-is-already-affecting-africa/.

Tomalin, Emma. "Religions, Poverty Reduction and Global Development Institutions." *Palgrave Communications* 4, Article 132 (2018): 1–12.

The United Nations. "Do You Know All 17 SDGs?" Accessed 29 July 2022. https://sdgs.un.org/goals.

Waltke, Bruce K. *Genesis: A Commentary.* Grand Rapids: Zondervan, 2001.

Walton, John H. *Genesis.* NIV Application Commentary. Grand Rapids: Zondervan, 2001. Kindle.

Watts, Rikk. "Making Sense of Genesis 1." *Stimulus* 12, no. 4 (Nov. 2004): 2–12.

Wenham, Gordon. *Rethinking Genesis 1–11: Gateway to the Bible.* Didsbury Lecture Series. Eugene: Cascade, 2015.

The World Bank. "Improving Gender Equality in Africa." 5 February 2014. https://www.worldbank.org/en/region/afr/brief/improving-gender-equality-in-africa.

Wright, Christopher. *The Mission of God: Unlocking the Bible's Grand Narrative.* Downers Grove: IVP Academic, 2006.

Wright, N. T. *The New Testament and the People of God.* Minneapolis: Fortress, 1992.

———. *Paul and the Faithfulness of God.* Minneapolis: Fortress, 2013.

Langham Literature and its imprints are a ministry of Langham Partnership.

Langham Partnership is a global fellowship working in pursuit of the vision God entrusted to its founder John Stott –

> *to facilitate the growth of the church in maturity and Christ-likeness through raising the standards of biblical preaching and teaching.*

Our vision is to see churches in the Majority World equipped for mission and growing to maturity in Christ through the ministry of pastors and leaders who believe, teach and live by the word of God.

Our mission is to strengthen the ministry of the word of God through:

* nurturing national movements for biblical preaching
* fostering the creation and distribution of evangelical literature
* enhancing evangelical theological education

especially in countries where churches are under-resourced.

Our ministry

Langham Preaching partners with national leaders to nurture indigenous biblical preaching movements for pastors and lay preachers all around the world. With the support of a team of trainers from many countries, a multi-level programme of seminars provides practical training, and is followed by a programme for training local facilitators. Local preachers' groups and national and regional networks ensure continuity and ongoing development, seeking to build vigorous movements committed to Bible exposition.

Langham Literature provides Majority World preachers, scholars and seminary libraries with evangelical books and electronic resources through publishing and distribution, grants and discounts. The programme also fosters the creation of indigenous evangelical books in many languages, through writer's grants, strengthening local evangelical publishing houses, and investment in major regional literature projects, such as one volume Bible commentaries like *The Africa Bible Commentary* and *The South Asia Bible Commentary*.

Langham Scholars provides financial support for evangelical doctoral students from the Majority World so that, when they return home, they may train pastors and other Christian leaders with sound, biblical and theological teaching. This programme equips those who equip others. Langham Scholars also works in partnership with Majority World seminaries in strengthening evangelical theological education. A growing number of Langham Scholars study in high quality doctoral programmes in the Majority World itself. As well as teaching the next generation of pastors, graduated Langham Scholars exercise significant influence through their writing and leadership.

To learn more about Langham Partnership and the work we do visit **langham.org**